Stand and Fight

Stand and Fight

Charles E. Miller

ISBN: Softcover   978-1-4535-9910-5
             Ebook   978-1-4535-9911-2

To order additional copies of this book, contact:
Xlibris Corporation
1-888-795-4274
www.Xlibris.com
Orders@Xlibris.com
87620

CONTENTS

PREFACE TO ESSAYS

There is a temporal quality to these essays, which means their substance is transient, related to the present Obama Administration. However, embeded in their thought are assurances of this nation's future and affirmation of the provisions, protections and constraints of the US Coinstitution. Therefore, I put them into print. It is always imperative that loyalists to this nation speak out, and I presume to have done so with these essays. They represent the resistance thinking of millions of Americans, another reason I proceeded wth their publication. They also constitute an implied warning against power-mongers who wish to control the lives of a free people, beyondf the protection and care of an omnipotent God, in whom our Founders believed and in whom they placed their trust in to annoint their labors in Philadelphia in 1789. I write, then with some perspective on history and insight into the problems that these essays refer to and attempt to correct. Freedom without God is anarchy because human justice supposes the secular control of fairaness, which is always flawed by human reasoning.

Man is fallible, even the most tyannical leaders commit errors mortal to the continuation of a great document, the fundamental law of a nation of three hundred million people, and the guardian of our hopes and visions for the future. This vision supposes a just people rather than a just State—the latter when man-centered being a liberal, Leftist premise—which inevitably presents the control of freedom by the introduction of laws of fairness. We are a nation of laws, and thus I write to indicate how the present tyranny, leading us in the wrong direction toward socialst controls, presumes to address our laws while at the same time isolating them with impunity and spending generations to come into bankrupcy on the theory that spending by the State liberates business enterprise. However, as experience proves, the liberation must come by way of expansion of the consumer base. The finest products and services in the world are of little value if the people lack the money to purchase them. Hiring more employees does not put money into the pockets of customers. For if that money comes from the Govenment, it is limited by the terms of the loan. Once gone, it is gone.

I have no compassion for the Tyrant who, as I have indicated, has taken over the fundamental law as if it were his instrument of personal regulatory opinion instead of law. And so he proceeds to the ultimate destruction of this great nation by the substitution of an alien ideology to replace our protective Constittion and our system of free enterprise. Insofar as these essays represent one citizen's rebellion against the tyrannical Central Government nowadays in America, I think they have been worth my efforts as one man's scrutiny of laws that he has lived under for many turbulent years. I have earned the right to rebuke the Tyrant. I have learned that First Amendment right by my reading of our Founders' work. Thus I present my rebellion in the form of these controversial essays, and I shall do lthe same with my vote.

THE GRAND TRANSFORMATION OF AMERICA BY GOD

The Obamacare bill "passed" by the House and announced by Neo-Marxist Pelosi as 220 to 211 is a fraudsulent piece of legislaion for two reasons:

1) It is a bill intended as a tax bill chiefly to raise revenue for the benfit of poiticians and trial lawyers. There is very little medical relief contained in the bill, certainly less than is now obstainable under our present system. The bill should therefore have originated in the House of Representatives, according to Article I, Section 7 of the US Constitution. "All Bills for raising Revenue shall originate in the House of Representatives . . . ."

2) The bill did not come as an exact text from the Senate, which is the scope and content and manner of lawful transmission from one House to thc other House. Art I, Sec 7: "Every Bill which shall have passed the House of Representative and the Senate . . . ." Another bill? One text only. It came, instead, as a presumed, a "deemed passed" piece of legislation. The House did not vote on the Senate Text. They voted on the Reconciliation bill, a composition of "fixes": to the Senate text. Therefore, the manner and configuration of the transmission was unlawful, deceptive, disingenuous and in violation of Article I, Section 7 of the Constitution. The House did not vote ont the Senate bill; they voted on the "fixes." The President sgned a bill that was never voted upon by individual Representatives in the House of Representatives. It is therefore fraudulent as legislation and subject to violations and to repeal, state by state under the Tenth Amendment to the Constitution. The power to make such a seizure of a major industry is not a power conferred upon or granted by law to the President or the Congress,

under the Constitution. Therefore each state has the right to challenge the bill's Constitutional legality under this Aendment X.

Even though House rules admit of a bill to be "deemed" to have passed, a Byrd rule for Budget recnciliations, the Senate bill came to the House illegally as a conciliatory statement of "fixes" or changes that were then "deemed" to represent the major healthcare bill. The House cannot deem a bill to have passed a major legislation, without a House (upper or lower) vote. Article I, Section 7. That corruption of a "deemed passage" wslithout a hand-count vote has yet to be challenged in the Supreme Court.

The bill was conceived and composed for politicians and trial lawyers, Obama supporters therefore the bill and its fraudulent passage betray

(a) Presildent Obama's antipathy toward he voting people of this republic, and

(b) a bribery of his supporters in both Houses to pass the bill regardless of the will of the people

(c) The people, by their vote express their assent or dissent from legislation. Thus, by the omission of the representative vote by the House, the bill remains unlawful and constitutionally irrelevant to the will of the people. Pelosi's perverse interpretation of "passed" to mean: "voted upon" by the House violates the letter and the spirit of the Constitution. She is not empowered to supervene in a hand-count by the House.

I would not hasten to endorse or encourage violation of Obamacare—not right away—because I do not sanction, at this time, the concerted violation of a legislative act. Rather, obedience is prescribed, keeping in mind that the way to (1) change the course of this bill's activation on the people is to vote the renegades out of office and (2) State by state to stand up to the Federal Government in opposition to what is by "process" an illegal and an invalid, nugatory and irrelevant piece of radical legislation. Le the Defnse show he Constlutional source of its authorty for Obamacare.

Remember, too, that our Founders did not devise, compose and pass the Constitution for the benefit of politicians, trial lawers, bureaucrats or any and all appointees of the Federal Government. It passed our Constituion in 1789 in a language that all literate persons can understand. It is a law by, with and for the people. Period. Therefore, any literate citizen has the legal, constitutional and historical standing to oppose Obamacare. This is our Country, not Washington's Remember that. Let me remind you of one thing, Citizen. If violence should come as an offshoot, a reaction, a passionate opposition by Americans to Obamacare, it will not be a civil or a piecemeal demonstration but will represent a people who rise up to put corrupt poliicians out of power. For it is power they seek, not leadership. By the seizure of power over our free society, they show contempt for America, these socialist-democrats. Like Obama, they wish to "completely transform" this country. If I changed into a grizzly bear, there will nothing left to remind others that I was once a man. That is his vision for Amerca. Obama's words were to "completely transform" America. There, by this logic, Barack Obama, Pelosi, Reid and the other complicit pirates are anti-Americans, throw in propagandists frothing meatball Chris Matthews and idiot Paperwad Keith Oberman as well. TRANSFORMATION IS A WORD OF TOTALITY, anything less than that totality is mere deception.

Remember, with regards to the violent opposition, that in 1775 we had an entire British army who had invaded our shores. Now, we have a civil opposition which, in the interests of keeping the fabric of this nation sound, whole and lawful, men of wisdom and discenment recommend against violence.

Also, do not forget that the bill is fraudulent for the above reasons; at best it is bad law and should be so considered. It can be repealed state by state, under Amendment 10 of the Bill of Rights, a power reserved to the States if not by enumeration given to the Government.

The Founders wrote the US Constitution chiefly for the people, their reading, their understanding, heir applicaion and their acceptance. Get it, Washington? This is our country. We do not serve you or your appointees or your radical destroyers.

LET ME BE CLEAR, AMERICA:

You can keep your own insurance policy
You can keep your own doctors—;
Let me be clear—

Insurers will be brought to heel

You will get tax credit for your policy

Small businesses will get get a tax credut for insuring their employees

Jobs will be created by the government

Those families with two or three children will receive tax credits

There will be transparency in my administration

I will totally eliminagte ear-marks

Insurerers can no longer raise skyrocket rates

Insurers can no longer reject pre-existing conditions, ulcers, paralysis, cancer

there will be fostered competetion between insurers that will reduce rates; government will enter the competition

Government will not cause the disappearance of favored insurerers' they will simply have to compete with single-pay Federal Insurance

Integrity will be our motto: no deception in government but transparency

Five hundred thousand new jobs (federal)

Every child a college education

Green energy will replace fossil fuels

Fraud, incompetence, waste and human error will abound. If you suppose that 300 millions citizens can function like a machine, all at once with virtual perfection, electronically, under the above fiats of Obamacare, you are literally stupid or irretrievably naive or mad in your denial of reality. Socialism involes the totality of sociey in absolute cooperation with mandates of the State. I'm told that Peons identured to the Central Government eventually get used to their chains. Kenyan and socialist Obama must absolutely reduce us to an abject third-world country if he even expects us to function according to the provisions of Obamacare and other agency policies like Cap and Trade. Remember, to "transform" as Obama promised signifies totality of change, as from man into a grizzly, a virtually classless nation into fifedoms of classes, a free people into obedient serfs, a democratic government into a tyranny, a free-trade economy into a totally regulated distribution of Centrally prescribed goods according to rationed "needs." Think about that, you 40% who see Obama as a reasonable facsimile of the risen Christ for this nation.

PRESIDENT OBAMA,
TRUTH DODGER

Barack Hussein Obama failed to connect the pieces of evidence in the Dutch to America Delta flight 253, therefore, I find him guilty of negligence in the performance of his responsiblities as President who is responsile for the security of this nation, and derelect in his performance as Commander and Chief of the armed forces. In both commands he has broken allegiance to his oath of office. The failure to connect the pieces of evidence is his failure, based on nothing more than a failure to brief CIA Chief Leon Panetta, his show of contempt for such non-golfing details, his lack of a normal person's curiosity, and his inept manner of getting at the CIA's "latest evidence of terorism directed against this nation." Barack Obama cannot fob this error off on any other member of his cabinet. He must face the charge of negligence in the performance of his duties as Commander and Chief, and as as protector of the Constitution and of the people whom he serves.

He cannot ignore what was evident to the world, yet he has attempted to avoid direct responsibility for the lapse in security for the Delta flight from Amsterdam. CIA chief Leon Panetta is equally responsible for his lapse in observation and/or for his failure to communicate the evidence to the President. Head of the Department of Homeland Security Janet Napolitano cannot truthfully claim that her security apparatus "works." It obviously failed in this case.

Barack Obama conceals his negligence by a pretended innocence of knowledge as the reason for the breech in security. CIA chief Panetta was his choice for chief of that agency. If they did not communicate, that is the fault of Barack Obama and Panetta alike. If the evidence, the killer's father's revelation of his son's radical jihadist bent, the one-way fare, paid in cash, no luggage, the Yemen's name—all p pieced togther constitutd the suspicious "unconnected" pieces of evidence, where was the the responsilble anti-terrorist action. Those pieces were all evident to Panetta. He, too, voided his oath of office by his failure (1) to act on the evidence and (2) to communicate with his Chief.

Why did Obama ignore all hints of trouble and pretend to be an onlooker, taken by surprise? He does not want to offend the world bankers of the Bilderberg Group, the Council on Foreign Relations, the Trilateral Commission all of whom—the world's bankers and political manipulators—see Obama as their New World Order puppet (and we "the people," as their slaves). Barack; Obama did not want to appear to be politicaly incorrect, thus his deception. He seeks to be the leader in "Global Justice." He would have us view the terrorist as a lonely young man disenchanted by his father's wealth. We are supposed to believe Obama's plea to bring to justice all those involved. Such ils lthe state of global interconnection nowadays that passes for diplomagtic relations but s, instead, politically correct bull crap!

The terrorist's intention was evidence by his failure to ignite the explosive. Obama pretends surprise. He pretends dissociation from the CIA evidence. He pretends to tell the truth to the American people. He lis a deceiver, a keystone-cop actor, a promoter of fake "transparency" n government.

President Barack Obama does not champion the best interests of the American people, except to exploit them like any politician, but he champions "World Justice" of a "New World Order" (superior to our Constitutional justice) controlled by the milti-billionaires of the Bilderberg Group, and their operatives in the Trilateral Commission. He pretends to champion the people. Wall Street was bailed out. What happened to over nine trillion dollars looted from the U.S. treasury in the process? A cap on Excutive salaries was a fraud to appease the gathering suspicions of the American people. Whereiln the Constitution is that power given to him?

Pretense is the name of Obama's socialist game. His campaign promises of transparency, 5-days to read a bill, etc. were rhetorical trilcks, devices, the skewing of language. World bankers are using him, gradually making the Congress ceremonial (their Health Care vote) as they increase their puppet's power viz a iz the office of the President. Wait until Obama's "civilian military force just as powerful, just as strong, just as well funded as the military" gets under way—a national police acivated by the BIODATA card for all citizens—and FEMA's construction of Camps for political Dissnters becomes apparent. You will see the induction of youths 14-28 into service brigades, (a mere 3 months) the Jungensbund of Fascist Germany come alive again. They will be brainwashed to detest our history and to hate historical America, accused of race-hatred and imperialism. There is aleady afoot in some middle schools the plan to start American hisory at the Civil War Reconstruction! The SPP (Security and Prosperity union with Canada and Mexico) is not dead, just dormant for a time.

The man is evil. Barack Obama is an ugly ingrate who trashed conract law at GM, who trashed dozens of dealerships which in some instances were the life-work of the entrepreneurs, he has shown his contempt for the "profit motive" many times—though he is a billionaire hypocrite—he knows not the struggles of the middle-income American, he is a danger too the future of America. The dumbed-down main-stream media continue to worship him like a god. He ignores Blacks, he crams his adminisrtation with crooks and nepotists and power-mongers, he lies again and again to the people, he breaks campagn promises, scorns transparency by secret deals, he ignores the truth, he fawns upon our enemies, chastens our friends, plays games with race, feigns a beautific innocence by his manner, brings lobbyists and moneyed supporters into his regime, dismisses God as irrelevant and would make the people servants of the State, starting at the second grade with an "obey me" video for the kids.

In a word, President Barack Obama is a fraud as a leader of the greatest society of Western Civilization, the target for radical Muslim jihadists, whom he would cozy up to. He has abused his power office so many times that he stands as a rebuke to our founding Fathers. He has created over 40 czars, czars to whom are imputed significant discretionary powers neither stated, implied nor tangential in Article II of the US Constitution. They are Czar bureaucrats who are not answerable to a Congress elected by the people.

Artiucle II, Section 2 in referrence to the Executive powers, reads in part: "He shall have the Power by and with the advice and consent of the Senate to make Treaties . . ." (SPP, NAFTA. Copenhaggen?) " . . . provided two-thirds of the Senators present concur . . ." (see the vacationing empty chamber) " . . . and he shall NOMINATE, and by and with the advice and consent of the Senate, shall APPOINT Ambassadors, other PUBLIC MINISTERS and Consuls, Judges of the supreme Court, and other Officers of the United States, whose Appointmns are not herein otherwise provided for and which shall be established by Law, but THE CONGRESS may by Law vest the Appointment of such inferior Offiers as they think proper in the President alone, in the Courts of Law, or in the Heads of Departments."

NOTE: the reference to Power in Article II, Section 2 is always back to THE CONGRESS, not to a singular kingship power possessed by the President. A one-party Congress may reduce the opposition but not eliminate the direction of the flow or transfer of that authority, or eliminate the constraints put upon that power. We have a Presiden who in his benign arrogance ignores the direction and the source of that authority. He preempts powers that by law belong to the Congress and, in effect, awaits their conciliatory affirmtion without proposal and concurrence. This overreaching of presidential power leads to a ceremonial ("rubber stamp") Congress who, like the British Parliament of king George III, agrees without disagreement to the king's proposals. I resent and rebuke the President for that overreaching abuse of Executive power. I, too, am a citizen of the Republic.

The President has the Power to appoint officers to carry out his and the Congress' assignments, not the power to impute to those officers (Czars) that they are totally at liberty to mandate their own non-statutory agency powers—without oversight, without a suckered-in mainstream media opposition. For example, as the FCC becomes more and more powerful and far-reaching, the Amendment I free speech right of Americans becomes increasingy threatened, minimized and manipulated as unimportant primarily to the government and less so to the people. Thereby, communications by the government to the people becoms empty rhetoric—see his promissory speeches—regulatory reflections of one-party Presidential Power. Already, the liberal, democrat brain-washed attitude engendered by the Omnipotent State has construed certain of the God's Ten Commandments as politically incorrect! The Supreme Court will prove to be commmplicit in removing God entirely from American society.

The direction of this increase in censorship is to make America a one-party system of government and therefore inevitably a dictatorship. To World-bankers money is the weapon of choice, the only way to rule out America's hedgemony of authority on the stage of a New World Order in which "global justice" will supercede Constitutional justice, the civilian trials of enemy GITMO combattants in NY, a political ploy, notwithstnding. Barack Obama has informed the world that GLOBAL JUSTICE is the desire of the American people. Such a monstrous fascistic lie ought not to go unopposed—though pleasing to globalist bankers (see European Bilderberg Group of 125 some-American Wall Street milti-billionaires). However, remember the cliche: the bigger the lie, the more readily it is accepted. The bigger the Govenmen in Washington, the more credible and legtimate it appears to be as our true heritage of 1789. especially in view of the "updatling" of the US Constitution by the leftists in the Government, especially in the Supreme Court. Constraints on the Executive powers and rules for making change in the Constitution are anathema, a curse, to Barack Husein Obama, outlaw.

BAIT AND SWITCH TO PASS OBAMACARE

You stick a gun in the face of the teller and order your pal to open the safe: That is a rule for robbery. The US Senate makes its own rules. Presently, the American people are under the Senate gun, held by Pimp for poltical prostitution Harry Reid;. The Robbers are the liberal Democrats who intend to rob you, the investors in America, of their wealth and priceless liberty. That is a Senate rule—to trick you in order to rob you. Or, in political lingo, to exchane an acceptable law for a dubious law at the time of the House vote, that is to say—to corrupt the vote by this fraudulent malpractice of bait and swiltch.

But that rule has another appearance. The Health Care bill that Congressman Reid has been "working on" will pass by reason of the operation of a house rule that is simply a bait—and-switch manipulation by Pimp Reid himself. He will hold the gun, a 2000 + page Socialist Healthcare bill that stands almost a foot high . . . he will get the Senate to adopt and "pass" this bill. Nobody has read it. It was not delivered until yesteday, Tuesday. Nobody understands it . . . lawyers. But the bill can be passed by reason of the Pimp's slight-of-hand that has become a rule for voting in the Senate (and in the House), a rule by which a favored bill is passed while he relies on it a controversial bill to the House. The House passes the favorable bill and because the controversial bill is a "rider" on the former legislation, the House deems the controversial bill to have passed. That is fraud. Damn the rule of rider legislation . . . usually concerning innocuous bills of finance.

Senator Harry Reid is a faudulent operator, as are a majority of Democrats in the Senate. Bait and Swtch wil consist of this: Present a lesser bill that grants benefits to Veterans. Hooray! Then, remove that bill and substitute the healthcare bill without telling; the Senators. Thinking they are passing the veterans bill, they will vote to pass the bill on the table. Meantime, Speaker Harry Reid has substitued the healthcare monster for the vets bill and the vote is to pass the bill before the Senate. The bill that has pased is replaced by the bill that is in danger of failing. It will pass readily. by reason of he fraud just committed by Harry Reid on the Senate and on the people of this great land. Baited by the Veterans billl, the House passes the controversail bill. Noboby, but nobody, in the Senate will have the slightest sound knowledge and understanding of the Reid bill. Is that procedure, if not deceit, fraud and dishonesty, a form of political madness that we will be paying for for generations? I that despicable deceit is abuse of power. Is that not malfeasance under the aw, the holdup robbey, Senate rule not withstanding. If I blindfolded a man and told him to sign a conract for the sale of his property, took his money and then called the deal honest and law-abiding, that would be a felony or at least a malfeasance, a fraud on my part.

The Congress, run by Democrats, has turned into a rotten piece of political junk who would even consider this piece of legalistic crap. The fraud of bait and switch will occur, count on it. Senators who vote for this bill, after the bait and switch fraud, are verifiably participants in a dishonest operation of the Congress. For they hve disarmed both their weaker colleagues and duped the American people. In doing so, they steal from the nation its history of freedom and opportunity and enterprise by stuffing Obamacare down the people's throats and commanding their silence or the imposition of heavy fines as penalties. The Congess has turned into a gargantuan charlatan that threatens to take over the; preservation of our freedoms. The pipsqueek cowardly media are greatly to blame for this internal destruction of America.

Article I, Section 8 of the US Constitution states: "The Congress shall have the power . . . to make all laws which shall be necessary and proper for carrying into Execution the foregoing Powers, and all their Powers vested for the Constitution in the Government of the United States, or in any Department or Officer thereof."

The Senate, like the House, makes its own rules. Bait and switch is a rule of the senate. It has been done before. (What voters knew that?) It will be done with the healthcare bill, initiated by Harry Reid, the cynical pimp for corrupted democrat politicians who, prostituting their office of trust, will vote to pass the Senate Bill without having read it or disclussed it or amended it. Congressman Harry Reid thinks the bill is a done deal, and this monster will pass, to the delight of that smiling, arrogant socialist deceiver in the white house and all the other crooks who mitigate the anxiety of trial lawyers, cronies, special interests and Federal unions, by their cooperating votes. It's ready to cast off . . . thus who doubts what I am saying?

That abuse of power, that fraudulent switcharoo of bills is a rule, like the rule for a bank holdup I just cited. The smiling face behind the gun will be Obama, the crook who robs this nation of a fundamental industy, its health care enterprises. He and his cohorts are the safe robbers. We are supposed to remain mute, confined to our dreams of past glory, in order to permit this sleuth for degeneracy, Barack; Hussein Obama and his pirates rob the people of one sixth of the GNP, and indebt the taxpayers not with 787 plus billions of baillout money, but one and one third thrillions in a debt passed along to three, four generations.

Senator Harry Reid is about to begin his holdup rule for robbing the people of their freedom of choice in health care. The Pirates in the Senate stand ready to vote blind, without understanding, comprehension, debate, opposition . . . just dumb silence of brutes . . . and crooks who want what they ;want, money and power. Money is the name of this bill. Big, big Money from th safe of the American taxpayers, the crooks who swirl the safe nobe and scoop out the moeny are our alleged representatives in both Houses.

I told you so. I knew I knew that the House would use the healthcare bill as a rider on . . . I thought then . . . on TARP. Like the Senate plans to do, they passed it with mindless concurrence. These monsters of confusion are vulnerble to instant Washington spin.

Mindless crooks, Liberal Senators are whoremongers for power and money and control of the people. And Harry Reid is about to pull his bait-and-switch act this week-end. A Senate vote without knowledge is tyranny over the people. One talk-show host said that Senator Harry Reid should be run out of Washington, DC on a rail, literally. I agree. And those who vote for his monstrosity of legalese and confusion and people-control should be driven from their desks into the yard with ;a shotgun at their backs, for they are robbing the people of their most priceless possession, their liberty of free choice in an area that affects them so intimaltely and dramatically and permanently—their health care.

I warn you: you will never reverse this vote for such a draconian change that robs Americans of the finest health care in the world. Neve, ever. You will never expunge its cruel demands for inferior care, its interminable waiting, its crushing taxes and its rationing ir lis rationing for early death and care-denial.

The bills, both House and Senate are evil. They reintroduces the slavery of cost-effectiveness of a person's medical care, built into the bill. Are you worth your hire to pick cotton in Islander Obama's cotton field. Your only value to determine your medical care is your monetary value to the State. The State. The State is almighty god—the Central Government run by plutocrat socialists, led by Obama. Your worth is monetary, no more, to determine your worthiness for care and in many cases your right to life.

How do I know. By comparisons of centralized care with individual-choice care and, most apparently, by the application of Senate malfeasance viz a viz Senator Harry Reid's fraululent trickery that demolishes our present health-care system. Harry Reid and the democrat crook-practitioners in the Senate, the safe-crackers, lack character. They are corrupt.

The demons of hell have been waiting a long time to destroy America. It is about to happen. For, with the control of the healthcare industry, the insurance industry, the car industry, the banks and the health-care industry, little more remains to control but the regulation t of the religion (industry?)

I warn you, if you pass this bill, you will run to daddy in Washington for almost everthing, including pemission to go out and play, With jealous eyes you will regard the savings of those who by their private means, diligence and chararacter did not succumb to the blandishments of Senator Harry Reid and the Democrat pirate-whores in Congress. Damn the veterans, damn the American people in their dumb "leadership" expectations.

FEDERAL HEALTHCARE JURISDICTION UNCONSTITUTIONAL

We are "fortunate" to have Constitutional lawyers in the House who are competent to decide issues within their jurisdiction. What category of jurisdiction, Mme. Speaker? Jurisdiction over persons, subject matter, Federal and State both original and pending? Which does the good dame mean?

The blank-cheque statement is worthless before the oath to support and defend the Constitution of the United States. Under Articie I, Section 8, clause 18, The Congress has the power "to make all Laws whch shall be necessary and proper for carrying into Execution the foregoing Powers and all other Powers vested by this Constitution in the Governmen of the United States or in any Department or Officer thereof."

Question: Where is the implication or command or constraint on liberty of advice appertaining to the healthcare welfare of the entire people either denoted, suggested, demanded or implied in the a;bove clause of the Constitution? I an a literate person, yet I cannot find that supervening and all-inclusive authoritygilven to the Federal Goernment to swab my throat or amputate my leg or conduct my heart surgery.

Therefore, the Government's command that I and other citizens take out health insurance—whether mandated from both houses or from one only—defies logic, reason and common sense as improper, unlawful and un-Constitutional. The Constitutional jurisdiction of said Powers does not empower either Congressmen or Senators to invent a supra-power not implied or granted by Article I, Sec 8, clause 18.

You Congressmen covet the power to control what is most vital and sensitive to the people—their personal health. You criminalize non-compliance by your denial of free choice, and your threats of imprisonment. What if the youthful citizen cannot afford either the $3,800 fine or the cost of a jail term and an additional fine? You would impose medicare edits that are injurious and destuctive to freedom in America. Your lust for oligarchal command that we shall to your will and judgement conform is evident in the health-care bill you present.

You do not understand it, nor will the people. Yet you thrust upon 300 million individuals the contempt for our present system, which we find adequate, all the while ensconcing your colleagues-in-law—the trial lawyers—in readiness to debase the Constitution, defraud the people of the truth about our care, and crush the life from the general citizenry with court penalties based on your ill-gotten notions of justice. Yo are convinced that any crappy law you hall inven is protecgted by the jusice of a virtuous Fedeal Government In short, you plan to encourage tria lawyers to grow fat upon the lives of medical practitioners, while you, like buzzards, will never be satisfied. This curse of darkness you intend to visit upon the American people with your Obamacare, you soulless giants of disesteem and pigmy intellect, Reid, Pelosi and radical leftists in both Houses of the Congress. You assume a status of superior intelligence that is demonstrated neither by your words nor by your actions. Your dull, small minds and corrupt intentions will destroy the gifted in this great Constitutional Republic. You radical leftists in the Congress and iln the Administration are a den of vipers!

Those laws, by the way, ladies and gentlemen of the Congress, were made solely for the proteciton of the people from the oppressive, destructive and unlawful use of power by officials in office, the which you repesent. You are certainly not the British Parliament of 1776. The US Constitution was not constructed for the benefit and aggrandizement of sitting elected officials or grasping bureaucrats, howsoever well intentioned. I am a student of men as well as of the Constitution. I am certainly not your huckleberry.

What are those foregoing Powers and all other Powers vested by this Constitution in the Government of the United States or in any Department or officer thereof? Do they suggest that Congreessmen are not to trust the people? Do those powers mock over two hunded years of our brilliant history of struggle and enterprise and freedom? Do such allege outside-the-law inventions cancel out pleadings by the opposition, namely, that the health care (and other monstrous legislation) is destructive to this nation? Indeed, do your privae practices as lawyers intrude upon your good judgement as elected officials? We, the people, are not your clients. That attitude, I suspec, is partly the case. We will, in fact, tell you arrogant sheisters how to run your office, and if you find this depresses your egomania and infringes upon your will to control the people, then get out and good riddance. Go ack to uyour private kingdoms of law practice. More civic-worthy men and women will replace you. Humility ia not your Zeitgeist.

To Mme Pelosi. I say that empowerments of "original" and/or of "pendant" jurisdictional control by House members, regardless of their legal education, is worthless, irrelevant and unlawful. They are gratuitous emoluments of her—and Senator Reid's—radical chosing. The Speaker of the House does not possess that "original" power, especially when standing before the last clause quoted above. She has not the authority to concockt a power and then to bestow that power upon any Congressman or Congresswoman, like a royal Madam, Queen of the realm. She thereby emboldens them with a jurisdictional aura they do not possess in generality. For the Constitution is very speclific in its grant to Congress of Parliamentary discretion to make any law lawful. (Parliament tried that with the Stamp Tax, the flint that ignited the powder of our Revolution. Brittons against Brittons.)

It was deliberately designed so in order that the people, fugitives from similar oppressive mercenaries in Europe, might live in freedom, the freedom to make their own choices about what is most intimate to them, their medical care. Have you ever heard of the plague, the black death, and the causal lack of standards of sanitation and cleanliness, about medically-induced bleeding to cure a disease, about phoney medicines called "elixirs of healing," about hypnosis healing, about healing magic, charlatans of medicine, and taking the cure in waters, and more? Obamacare would return to this country some of these delusions of good medical care. Like phoney medications, quackery treatment and the black art of political persuasion that Uncle Sam is taking care of you and your children. The radical elitists in Washingtontake you for dumb and ignorant idiots. Beling power-gabbing charlatans, they are convilnced that they are right inthis magter of your halthcare. They are delusional and idolatrous of their power, beyond the constraints of Constitutional law.

Trusting in God as they did for their welfare and their very survival, that included good health, they fled old vassal-state Europe. Imitating the prince of deception, our President would turn you to imitate old Europe by his collaborationist (leftists in Congress) elimination of enlightened medicine in the US.
Furthermore, we who will be the alleged "beneficiaries of said bestowal have a right to reject that power because we are neither subjects of the Obama crown, nor are we vassals of the Federal Governmen-State. If we do so, let it be said that we—not all conservatives, by the way—rebel with intelligence and comprehension. We are citizens under the laws of the land. No Congressperson has an INHERENT right to override the circumscribed power of his his or her office in order to effect a law, a change in a law, a provision added to a law, a consequence of a law, an re-interpretation of a law, a personal application of a law, a new law without debate, discussion or a vote of the House. A seat in the Congress is not the same venue as member-management of a law firm. We are not your clients, you arrogant lawyer who intend to radicalize our democracy with some sort of sis-boom-bah Marxist cant of medical care! Keep in mind that you are our servants . . . servants of the people. If that galls you, find another job or go back to your law practice. You are adept at taking a side, one or the other, the prosecxution or the defense. But you are unsuited by your experience to ascertain, with honesty, probity and discernment, the common-sense aspects of a medical problem. You are therefore unsuited to medically diagnose and treat an entire nation of the hurt, sick and disabled. That is what your Obamacare bill implies. You assue a cogent relationship to medical science.

Poitical skimmer Mme. Pelosi's attempt to empower Constitutional lawyers in the House (Reid in the Senate) with non-existent power, for to to impose a presently moot law without its formal introducion is illegal and unlawful. That breech of existent statutes will come to light eventually. Her intent is not to urge "Constitutional lawyers" to observe proposals in their respective committees but, instead, to propose, and essentially to promise, laws which will override the inherent democratic perspectives of relevance, balance of opinion, her proposal of legislation being effecitve by virtue of the lawyers's expeience and training. It is not Madam Speaker Pelosi's office to cause a possible law to conform to the wishes of a radical leftist president—to the prejudice of the will of the people, no matter how celestial the law. One

cannot ethically talk about Obamacare as if it were already the law and
needed but brush-up touches to improve upon it. That spin is unethical
deception and it is intellectually dishonest.

The following are the Constitutionally authorized venues of power-to-control
for Constitutional lawyers, and others in both Houses.

Taxes, duties, excxises
defense
regulate commerce
naturalization
coin money
fight counterfeiting
piracies
war and supporting legislation
militia
control of DC

HEALTH CARE FOR THE PEOPLE . . . ? Is that empowerment actually
there? No. not without a Constitutional Amendment! The people have a
right to disobey the Federal Government in this connection.

I see no specific law that empowers the Congress to demand that the people
sign up for, accept Federdal control of, bear the cost and the regulations of, or
conform to threats of imprisonment and fines thereof, or subject themseles
to regulations imposed by the Congress for the mangemen and acceptance
of medical care for their personal health. Pelosi and the other leftist liberals
who plan to force the people, like British subjects of the king, not citizens
of a Constitutional Republic, to bend their knees to the Federal law of
Obamacare. The Leftists are asking for trouble from the people. Ameicans
are not prepared to abandon their great heritage like cowards in the face of
danger. This is especially true when we realize tht Pelosi, Reid, and other
far-left liberals skim money from bills into their personal accounts, buy
the votes of Congressmen who want to pinch and sniff at a law, and fawn
upon lobbyists who gamble fortunes to block the will of the people. What
are you running there in Washington, you Poltroons of spending graft and
chicanery? You betray the people in your will to follow that European Fraud
in the White House. I think it was C.S. Lewis who decried your sort as
"men without chests."

CHARACTER OR COWARDS

Some of you delegates may wonder about America's "cause and character," as Obama put it, in his UN speech before the General Assembly. (I could not find it in the official printed version to be relayed to the media.) President Obama used his 9-motnhs in office to illusrate this Nations "cause and characer." Nine months and he lectures us in our inimitable range of experience and in our yrars!

He left out the America's sacrifice of hundred of thousands of her fine young men lost in wars around the world, to secure liberty to others under the gun, murdered and terrorized by foreign dictators. That is character! He omitted the food programs, the huanitarian aid America has given to war-torn nations and peoples smashed by natural calamitie, sunamis, volcanoes and earthquakes. That is character.

Hc forgot to mention the brilliant gifts of science, industry, and technology we the American people have given, to the rest of the world often without compensation That is character.

He omitted our reception of the poor and the hungry and the outcast fugitives from oppression, lawfully, onto America's shores. That is character.

Instead, he covertly offered as exemplary of America's character titanic Federal spending in the trilions of dollars that threatens to bankrupt America and to imprison the intimate lives of its citizens in the Fascis State while they continue to "play by the rules" of good citizenship. That is character! He has already occupied the car industry, banks and insurance companies by raw seizuret, setting up a potential dictatgorship through FEMA while we show respect for our representatives' actions. That is characgter and cause!

Governed by an elite class of Czars and political appointees under his adminstration, he pleads that America has failed to share with the world—a blatant and undisguised lie—since we share nothing with Iran or North Korea that we want to embrace as ours.

Here is a short list of charcter novelties President Obama has introdcuced into our economy and our culture: (1) political pay offs (2) bribes, (3) favortism toward special interests like the Labor Unions and the trial lawyers (no tort reforem), (4) Media control-propaganda, (5) hidden gifts to avorite Congressmen and abettors to his presidency, like ACORN; (6) golden parachutes allowed retring CEOs, like his Chief of Staff and (7)_ Higher taxes demurred but on the way. Americans need a lecture on characer?

This nation has sacificed more blood in the cause of liberty and liberating peoples from dictators and death by starvation, torture and the gun, than has any other nation in human history! That ils character!

Mr. President, you don't fool millions of Americans who have read and lived through America's's courageous and character-girded history down through our 230 years of existence. What's more, you will not change it by attempting to expunge that great history—through your cowardly global apologies and appeasement before evil men—in order to promote your warped, desperate, fallible and proven-unworkable system of the justice and opporunity that will fails to evolvee. Never for us, sir. And if you impose martial law upon us because the Congress refuses to pass your health care bill, the Waxman monstrosity, I for one will spit in your face as a Normady veteran of WW II. (Loyal Frenchmen did the same as the Nazis marched down Paris' Champs de Elysees.) Clear?

Let me give any happenstance readers of the above a couple of hor d'euvres in the poetic vein.

THE OPPRESSIVE CHEAT

A shallow cheat his sullen curse supplies
Aloof, crimp'd men's will, dire fate demamds.
Yet thwart his writs he hasty spreads cruel lies
To make men's life his own by 's strict comanads.

Our kindlier ways he condemns. he vain tolls
Dear thoughts, words, venues become our trial
For his censures are his tyrant force to scroll
Whilest he adds his measures' dark concealed guile.

This Caesar of the days makes men's court his goal
To clone them in choice rapture 's foul'st schemes
All he squanders of men's wants he finds droll.
Who ken his might, to quench their privy dreams.
He makes of us his clone, his will he foists
As all we do and say condemn his voice.

HOPE MADE DREAD

Masters he the innoc'nt to fetch his will
Who pleads their case before appeal in need.
Yet. beggars he men's kindlier hope to fill
Whilest he curries tyrants' hate to join their creed.

Poltroon, he comes 'to power by common kind
Who vote for favor, refrain from conscience stil.
His office he grasps to make men mockeried blind,
He scams them quick to find in honor figment's shill.

Alas, all faith goes with 's caponed signal lies,
He leaches death by votes to augment 's end

That makes of better grace a trusting surmise
And culls vain hope unto his sworn disguise.

Hailed, this rotting gamster mocks a kindlier fate
To make his barin th' scoped out trammeled slate.

CIVIL TRIAL FOR JIHADIST
WAR CRIMINALS

The shootng at Camp Hood was commtted by a Jihadist Muslim as an act (1) of obedience to Allalh's command to kill the infidels, and (2) as a response to military separation of radical: Muslims from "infidel" GI's.

Charles Krauthammer has stated in his column that lierals regard the multiple murders and woundings as (1) the result of medicalization, and therefore (2) the Sheik is a "viltim" of "medicalization," ie. drugs.

Lacking to this concept are (1) perpetrators and (2) motives. Perpetrators can be the pressures of a profession and the patient to patient confidences shared with the Major at Walter Reed Hospital and in camp.

A profession can influence a man to such an extent that it generates feelings of retribution. But others shed similar experieces as returningf veterans, therefore that thesis does is not valid or ethical.

Patient confessions can generate resentful, even violent feelings, but self-discipline should control any impulse to violence. This is especially true in the light of other clinical workers sharing the same experience with vets.

Now we reach the ultimate conclusion, that if the perpetrators of a crime against a "victim" in this case the Major, it can be inferred that the self-condemnation of the Major was a part of the post stress syndrome ("medication"), and therefore patient confessors ("returning stressed vets") cannot be accused of harboring a desire to murder the "victim" or cause him to murder others. Thus, the only powerful violence—generated factor was Sharia Law.

That law is apparently embraced by the "victim" Army Major. That, I think, is the discernable truth of this case. The causal factor(s) are not post-traumatic stress and/or that he "broke down" or he was a treatable "nut case." ("medication") These politically-correct, erroneous judgements are held by by liberals media, the Time Magazine and the NY Times. The Major was never deployed.

Those quasi-medical judgements mislead from the truth. They lack the wisdom of truth and that is silenced to defend the judges from charges of anti-Muslim religious bias. Such moral cowardice can possibly result in a hand-off treatment of the murderer. He will be exonerated from the murer of 13 ilnnocent soldiers and wounding of 31 other Camp Hood soldiers, in order to give him medical treatment. That compassion is unrealistic, politically correct, evasive, maudlin in its sentimental feelings, cowardly and jeopardizing of the safety of others under the same ruberic of "innocent by way of mental aberration." No "Twinkies" this time.

Count on it: in another case, the Muslim five Gitmo detainees soon to be tried in a NY Federal Court will plead innocent for lack of witnesses (3,000 dead witness from the grave), and innocent for for lack of (battlefield) evidence.

Declared innocent, they will then sue the people for false imprisonment—to be treated as US citizens innocent until proved guilty (4th Amend.). Their Defense will stress—"deprived of life, liberty, or property without due process of law" under (V), and each man will complain of being forced to "witness against himself." and under (VI)—point to the 8-year lack of a "the right to a "speedy and public trial". under (VIII)—meantime, sufferilng "cruel and unusual punishment, All of these Constitutional protections for the Amercan citizen can be entered as arguments to free the accused Jihadists, having been given "due process of law."

NOTE: just as there is no statement in the first Ten Amendments to our Constitution about a "wall of separation" between the State and religion, so is there no statement that a man (in this case the terrorists) are "innocent until proven guilty." DEFENSE OF THE GITMO 5 WILL APPEAL TO

PC AND TO FEELIGS. Fools will defend the murderers in and outsdie the court. Fools will believe them. Because they come from a Theocracy, thy will charge the American court with violation of the sacred Koran and therefore hold our justice in contempt and denegration.

POWER—SEEKERS ABOUND

I derive many of following truths and concepts from Rousas Rushdoony's book "Christianity and the State." Consider this letter a book review of Dr. Rushdoony's very excellent and enlightening exposition of the hostility of God toward the un-righehteous State. My contribution is the appliation of his concepts. Romans 13 predicates a righteous State, God's agent and minister, that operates within God's will, the which evil-doers should fear when they fail to "subject" themselves to the righteous State, that is, to obey the laws of their society. That was the State envisioned by America's Founders. Their vision was not athleocracy but a secula; State whose leaders respeced the law, honored God and practiced honest dealings with the people. Our leaders today envision a secular, globalist God-denying State that excludes the faith of our forefahers, eliminated God from schools, public forums and State recognition while at the same time, they admi satanist worship as legitimate relgious worship and expung the name Jesus: from the ministries of all chaplains.

The "completely transformed" State—from liberty to oppression, from individualism to masses conformty, from enterprise to submission, from opportunity to Statist regulations, from productivity to entitlement—contemplated by Marxist. Radical Obama ils currently hoping to acquire total power, disguised as relativstic compromise with our history and our laws, a dictatorship of the Presidency. To this end, Obama, Pelosi and Reid have arrogated sovereignty unto themselves, finding it expedient to trick the people into acceptance of Obamacare without a House vote of the Senate bill for Obamacare. The vote was for a "reconciliation" of the Senate bill the Senate bill being "deemed", or raher presumed" to have passd . . . WITHOUT A HAND—COUNT OF HOUSE VOTES FOR THE SENATE BILL. To "deem" a bill as having passed is a substitute for an actual vote on a bill the text of which must remain unchanged and identical when passed between the two Houses. To "deem" is not to vote. To deem is to presume agreement and that is fraud of a major piece of legislation. Passage was, therefore, outside the purview of the US Constitution. The; House rule of presumptin is not intended for such a monumental piece of legislation!

But by using this device, which changes one-sixth of the US economy, the Congress usurps. abuses, oversteps the power of the Constitution, which has total sovereignty to determine and to control the course of this nation of laws. The Constitution! radicals scream . . . what a ploy to avoid reality Reaity? Americans have yet to experience the destructive costs of the deemed Obamacare bill. To suggest God's role in our government sounds irrelevant to the pragmatic matter of Constitutioal passage of the legislation. I am not silent as to the ultmate consequences but I say, at this time, that such a device of trickery—the House can make its own rules—augers the destruction of a nation by default. We will all suffer in that destruction, which will result from the "transformation" by the piratical seizure by the White House scheme. What else can you call boarding the car industry and with sabre flashing, tearing contractual laws apart? All three boarding pirates of the Regime were involved in the fraudulent deemed "passage" of the Obamacare bill. They were in fact, the conspirators of a despicable fraud against the people.

Do you see any humility in their magisterial words to control the people by fraud and precedural manipulation? Small wonder Obama demeaned "process." Obmacare was "passed" by a deception of the people Be aware that when the State by example, choice and ignorance eliminates God's providence from its customs, values, laws and traditions, it becomes the source not just of all power but of counterfeit ethical andmoral virtue. The State has then empowered itself to enforce conformity and uniformity in the cause of ethical "fairness.". The virtuous State, without any other reference than itself, can then deterine the kind, extent and expression of its own power. The State ean do no wrong. That is Washinton's attitude today. Those given un-Constitutional powers, a the 39 Czars and the cabal of stooges for Obama will autocratically and alone, judge what is and is not "fair." Because it is absolutely virtuous, the State will determine what is criminal, wrong, unjust and illegal and thus thus the government in DC, will establish its closed system of humanistic values at which man is the center. The State is then. by its own self-declaration—qualified by judicial consent to try war criminals as civilian lawbreakers with its perfect justice. There is no higher power. The State becomes the source of virtue. Churches, religion, home training are all irrelevant and must be allowed to atrophy in the New Age of globalist America.

Dishonesty is virtuous when the means justfy the end. Freeing prison inmates is virtous if the act will balance the budget. Taking from one man, his home, his business to give to another citizen—by eminent domain without domanic values—is virtuous if that other "needy" person lacks a home, a business, a hard-working income. This transfer o f wealth is called an entitlement by the radical present Admlinistration. The seizure of private property togive toanother private person becomes a virtuous act in the eyes of the virtuous State. It is virtuous politically to brainwash kids in the grades by White House videos because those kids will later become productive socialist citizens as a result of having been brainwashed to produce for Uncle Sam.

It is virtuous to destroy the notion that captal is wise, prudent, advantageous, and risky, because capitalism is the anathema of fairness in a democracy where all are equal. It is virtuous to control medical doctors but not trial lawyers, because the benefits to the former are rooted in greed but the trial lawyers practice a degree of fairness in their causes of action that benefits all of society. Whereas a surgery may be botched—the false fear behind lack of tort reform in Obamacare—a trial for equity brings rewards to the deprived. That is "fainess" in action. A the sole souce of virtue, the State can therefore do no wrong.

As its powers increases, the State's zeal to penalize dissent increases. We see that today, wherein a Senator will attempt to cut off dissent by punishment in one form or another. We see that today in the cowardly silence of the media to expose Washington retribution against dissent. Penalties can consist of jail, fines, illicit (expedient) taxes, disdainful laugher by the President, mockery of the people and denegration of the nation's history. These are all devices of the tyrannical State. It is morally wrong to replace the courts and legislatures with violence and open revolution. It is expeditious to see the benevolent Rulers focused on expanding government power in order to control the people's lives and, according to Marx, spread the unjustly-acquired wealth not just to Americans but to the resj of the "suffering" world. The, the people, will become the slaves and footstools to this process of change.

Propaganda! Already, the mainline media are literally the propaganda arm of the Obama administration.

Barack Obama is attempting to create a class—society of controllable workers for and under the heel of the government as receivers of the government's largesse. I am convinced that he intends to crush the wealthy and middle-class into one, undefineable mass of entitlement recipients, docile before the new god of the State, and happy and contented to receive the provisions of a central government that is evil in its intent and pratices. I'm waiting for a Minister of Information, a Goebbels of propaganda, to emerge and be named an Information (Propaganda) Czar. Is it already the Press Secretary?

By making their authority absolute, the Rulers become an abomination in God's eyes. They usurp the will of a righteous people, in complete contradistinction to Romans 13, that promises a righteous government and an obedient people who need not fear the State unless they do evil. Without God the State is the determiner of its own power. According to Romans 13, the State is the minister of God. When, however, the State presumes to be our material and implicitly our spiritual savior, it transgresses God's law and becomes evil. Salvation from what? From needs, from the injustice of wealth-seekers, and from the unfairness inherent in our history. When, in effect, the State becoms the total provider of our human needs, it usurps God's role in human intercourse and practices evil; (God! Ask God for food stamps!) The government becomes evil when State promotes its salvic power, salvation from evil, salvation from death, salvation from immoral acts . . . as defined not by Scripture but by the corrupt will of the Marxist State and the rulings of a manipulted Supreme Court. Gone will be conscionable acts by the government and by the people. Gone will be true justice but rather. in its place, the advent of mediocre society in education, medicine, business and local administration. Gone will be the competition that elevates an exposes superiority in work, product and ambition.

At this point the State replaces the church, replaces religious faith and establishes itself as the arbiter of morality, virtue and justice and without God the inventor of laws to suit its own will. That is anarchy. A man has the right to the fruits of his own labor? No, the State has that rght—Obama's State—and, seizing those fruits, he will redistribute them according to its doctrine of "fairness." That is Europe's godless, mediocre and unproductive environment.

The State, i.e. government is God's agency for the welfare not of the Rulers but of the people. Thus Obama's agenda is for the welfare of the Rulers—leftists, trial lawyers, union supporters, lobbyists. enjoyers of taxpayer bailout emoluments—and not for the welfare of the people. The Government, i.e the State is today a Godless entity. We can, therefore, expect it to lie to us, to cheat on the people, to innovate laws that break the Constitution, to seize powers delegated to the other branches, to indebt the people for four gerations and by trickery and obfuscation eventually wipe out the Bill of Rights thereby, purging personal freedoms in the bill of Rights, while ultimately destroying our great country. The cowardly silence of the "free press" is a Federal indulgence. The media no longer has a soul. They re a ridiculous joke. "Truth, what s ruth?" the media ask, like Pontius Pilate at Christ's trial. Truth is what Barack Obama says it is. N'est pas?

Man was not created in the image of the State but in the image of God. Therefore Barack Hussein Obama is first answerable to God. As the State, the usuper dies—that despite all signs to the contrary—man's responsibility for his actions and his freedom will increase. For there comes the death of freedom whenever man becames god. The modern humanistic State is a jealous god and will tolerate no contending rivals. Indeed, it indulges in immorality (see lies, scandals, back-room deals, bribed votes in Congress) and tolerates no moral declarations, actions or presumptioms of independence and individualism among the people under its control. In fact license given to immoral acts, as plunderingingof the txpayers, by the State's subtle, unspoken sanctions engenders a fear from which the State promises protection. Thus we will witness the growing tolerance for immoral conduct among the citizens as a means of Statist fear-control.

Accompanying that tolerance for immorality among the popuace comes an increase in taxes to contlrol same—a fraud—and a lessening of true government alongside ever-increasing power. When a State becomes prophetic of the future, it assumes the role of Jesus Christ and the church. As the State becomes more powerful, it increases its pressures to conform and to become uniform . . . in today's language—to be fair. It is politically-correct to endorse a mindless "fairness," but nobody knows exacly what it means! To give awards to people who have not earned them? To make sure that no family has to make a sacrifice greater than another in or to have a successfu marriage, to acquire an education . . . ? Fools! Obama's attempt to "transform"

America into a Utopian nation of enforced euality will bring this nation crashing down economically. We are not all equal, Charlatans.

Note: that with the increase in power comes less true government (benevolent abstention, cautious intervention, caring regulation) and more taxes. We are in that broiler today. Obamacare is not governmen at its best. It is Statist compulsions through taxes to benefit the bureaucrats and leftists in the administration and in the Congress. The goals of the authoritarian State are control, regulation, jurisdiction and power. The control is established in order to authorize the Rulers to manipulate the economy and all institutions that contribute to that economuy. With that control comes the power to invent new laws, break the basic Constitutional law, judge the citizens without charges and usurp power from existing branches of government. \

Obama legislates, Obama silences the Court and invents (legislates) Czars with (autocratic) powers not granted to them by the Constitution. He is, in effect, an outlaw in charge of the government, smirking at and mocking the people who put him there. He is a fraud, an incompetent, a radical manipulator, a ne'er-do-well from chicago's machine politics. He promotes disharmony in order to justify invented-law changes in government. His 39 Czars bathe in invented powers over the people. Talk about legislating from the bench! Barack Obama legislates from the oval office!

When the State becomes a terror to good men, it has ceased to merit obedience. (Rushdoony) 1 repeat. When the State becomes a terror to good men, it has ceased to merit obedience. Remember that. And when under these circumstances religion is merely tolerated, it is not free. It is allowed to exist by fiat, condesension, tolerance of the all-powerful State. It is therefore subject to removal, cancellation and condemnation by the State. As the salvationist State becomes the agency of providence, it replaces God. When the State can do no wrong, the citizen's freedom is illusory. Under these circumstances of the inculpability of the State, the citizen has no right to differ with the State, that is, to differ by any attempt to oppose a provision that has been secretly embedded in Obamacare, as the Biodata card. It bears repeating that when the State acts to replace God in the minds of the people, it becomes the providential replacement for God to control the actions and especially the thoughts of the people. In short, resistance is made to appear unfair, unlawful, and anti-social—the croaking of the Leftists—because individual thought as a matter of dissent are contrary to the "wisdom" of the State. All resisance is therefore hostile to the omnipotent socialist State, regardless of what the Conservative-traditionalist resists. Dissent is made ot appear seditious! In order to insure "fairness", by the pressures for conformity, compliance and uniformity. then responsinle expressions of honesty in Rulers of the all—powerful State are no longer God's command but becomes a human utility. an expedient act, a politial—correctness Adoration of the State and is Rulers becomes politically-correct in all vnnues of public expression, including the pulpet.

Therefore bald-faced lies are permitted in order to advance and to enlarge the State because lies are useful to the promotion of ever greater power control of the people. Again, the end justifies the means. By ruling out God in public discourse, by attaching fines to expressions of faith in public throught, by trivial court rulings, by punishing Christians, the State asserts its humanistic, absolute power. In order to legitimize Obama's lies as truth, the State is compelled to consider the common people as stupid and ungrateful and, as a shibboletlh of Marxism, they, Amerians, are the illiterate (European) "unwashed masses."

Our ignoramus-of-history President is a consummate liar. His words and his actions are not to be trusted. It follows then that to legitimize his lies about his agenda, he literally must in his absolute authority—by his actions—transgressive of God, consider the people as incapable of caring for themselves. Therefore, he urges us, the people, to thank him as god—a whimper he has expressed in his most recent dishonest judgement. I say again, that he is not to be trusted either his words or his actions. Having grown up in Hollywood, I am innoculated against his smiley, smooth-talking sort of charisma. I honestly believe that my highschool education in the 1940's exceeds his collegiate training at Harvard!. I learned the value of character and the meaning of truth-search and I learned to think. He has learned none of these. Karl Marx, Alinsky and his leftist piratical crew do the thinking for him. Leftist Idealogue Obama offers opinions as searching thought to the people. Cheers!

CONSEQUENCES OF OBAMACARE

I have spent a number of years in the medical profession, working with and caring for patients, opening their charts to examine diagnoses and prognoses, and having compared notes with other workers alongside of me, I can attest to the validity of these consequences, as I foresee them, now that Obamacare is "deemed" to have passed both Houses.

1. Creates doctor shortage—many will leave profession or retire early

2. Creates rationing of care as result of shorages (see # 33)

3. Dangerous control of hospital beds, services, staff members and qualifications

4. Overtaxes insurance companies, costs passed on to patients and bankrupts taxpayers.

5. Overtaxes taxpayers to support care program. Will impoverish taxpayers.

6. Invites foreign doctors, nurses with poor training therefore inferior care

7. Crushes auxiliary industries: medical aids as machines, wheelchairs, etc,

8. Drives support businesses out of business, commercial laundries, delivery systems

9. Reduces availabiity of critical medicines because of FED control

10. Encourages black market in drugs, and introduces importation of unprotected and impure drugs from UK Canada, China, India

11. Encourages illegiimate store-front surgeries by quacks that will, inevitably, result in death from infection and botched surgeries.

12. Encourages fraud within all areas of medicine in US

13. Prompts death-with-dignity providers . . . and resultant suicides

14. Limits admission hospitals and clinics to those politicaly qualified for care.

15. Punishes non-participants with heavy fines $3800., usually the young and healthy

16. Produces long waiting lines for almost any care at all. Numerous will go untreated as a result of having to wait weeks, months, sometimes years for treatment.

17. Produces deaths due to long waiting times for critical surgeries and medicinal care.

18. Produces a predictable plethora, quantities of errors in transmission of medical advilce, misinterpretation of files, wrong medications, confusion as to diagnoses, confusion as to which patient is subject of transmission, mixups with same names, general foul up of communications between attending doctors and Washngton.

19. Loss of confidence in medical care in America

20. Destruction of legitimate and time-honored doctor-patient relationship.

21. Scrambling and confusion of files on every living person in the US. Careless dependence on electronic transmissions., including mistaks at keyboard as to dosage amounts, kind of surgery, right or left appndage,.

22. Perversion and corruption of medical science because of a lax an ill-motivated dependence upon foreign knowledge as better than ours and dependence on corrupted laboratory tests as diagnostic truth.

23. Lack of nmnvations in pharmaceuticals that have produced wonder drugs.

24. Lack of inventions in critical medical aids, like the MRI machine, cardio-pulmkonary machine, the sterizizing audoclave, special lights for surgery, monitors for patient surgical and critical-care surveillance, etc. You have removed profit, the reward for diligence, the inspiration for future improvements in care and all things related thereto. The entire system will begin to run down, in need of replacments and repairs.

25. Much sufferilng of patients' loved ones because of any of the above.

26. Shoddy workmanship in surgery. Indifference in care induced by sheer distance from central, bureaucratic controls of care.

27. Poorly maintained hospitals and clinics, as in Cuba. Dirt infection, disease carried by unsanitary clinics hospitals. This includes cockroaches, rats, unmonitored germs at sinks, toilets, beds, etc. Money lacking, as for roads and bridges.

28. Loss of spiri;ual contact, hospital chaplains non-existent. A thoroughly Godless system.

29. Fall off of voluntary care because of conditions and indifference, distance and irrelevance of care from Washington, DC Doctors no longer make critical-care decisions but now follow orders. as employees of the State.

30. Closing of hospitals and clinics because of lack of operating funds, taxes no longer sufficient, just as illegals have forced hospital closures because of FED hands-off policy.

31. Clossure of medical schools and training facilities because of lack of students, money and calls to a failing profession. Inferior quality of medical candidates for training.

32, Ominous health care rationing. In Baucus Bill 683 m Section 9 three is a statement to the effect that a doctor appointed and/or approved by the Washington Secretary (Ezekiel Emanuel) has an Incentive not to utilize care for a certain patient. NOTE: that decision although politicaly motivated is not necessarily medically appropriate to the case, a crucial disconnect that can readily condemn the patient to death. That means rationing and highly selective care approved in Washington, DC by the Medical Secretary and his Board of Bureaucrats. This kind of control over the care of one patient is control over the care of all because the care is centrally contolled.

33. Obliteration of the world's finest medical system. May this sweeet plum turn to ashes in your mouths, you Obamacare devotees who would promote single-pay as the silver bullet for medical care for an almost insignificant percentage of the population.

34. Widespread bribery by Sen. Reid to bring moderates and douters to heel. Ex: Reduce excistax on medical devices, grant outright Sen. campaign monies, mak promises unfulfilled until bill passes. Machivellian Reid will do almost anything to gain a passage vote.

LET ME TRY A DIFFERENT TACK:

THESIS: doctors will work for a set salary, like VA employees
ANTITHESIS doctors who spent great sums of money for their Specialized training will not willingly surrender their talents, earning-capacity, pride to Obamacarc,

THESIS: There will be no critical nurse shortages:
ANTITHESIS s: Nurses must be trained, they are not day laborers, and, unlike Presildent Obama, they do not and cannot take on-the-job training.

THESIS: Fixing numbers of beds and size of hospital occupancies is a cost saving step.
ANTHESIS Bed availableilty cannot be determied on a first come, first serve basis and still accommodagte patients waiting, some critical surgery. Field hospitals as in combat, will have to be set up to care for the many. Emergency needs cannot be computerized without coverages. Overflow subject to beds in tent wards.

THESIS: fixing caps on insurance rates will teach insurers to be honest
ANTIHESIS: Charley Rangel's bribery of hias ethics committee members to overlook his tax indiscretions explodes that honesty "in the first place" quirk of Obama.

THESIS: Health s insurance rate schedules will fine-tune consumer discretionary spending habits. The Cost-effectiveness of those rate schedules will smooth out Obamacare. Motice hypocite Obama's discretionary thrift with Milchell's fashion trip to Paris and his junkets around the world, not to mention Pelos;s giant 747 200-seat flight every week to California. The people are not your servants, you cheats!
ANTITHESIS: You cannot fine-tune the care costs for a horrible car accident, the crippling effects of polio, tuberculosis and other long-term care events in the individual/s life.

THESIS: He's too old to expend money on. Let him die a naural death.
ANTITHESIS: Thes system will wipe out discoveries of new wonder drugs and other findings of medicine we now enjoy that extend human life. Count on it. Not immediately, but iu time, longivity will become a thing of the past except for those who are genetically predisposed. Longivity will be scorned as detrimental to the masses, at which time euthanasia will be regarded as an alternative. Virtually every great sciemtist, statesman, artist, musician, preacher was "old" by Obama's standard of age . . . 50 plus. Human experience will be regarded with suspicion because it is connected to age . . . like our old, white-haired Founding Fathers.

THESIS: The new system will be honest, with safeguards.
ANTITHESIS: Oh, and what exactly are those safeguards to fraud and corruption, crooks like Charley Rangel chairman of the Senate Ethics committee, a tax evader and brilber par excellence?

THESIS: Socialist health care rationing will eliminate many problems occasioned by greedy doctors who over treat and over medicate and ovecharge.
ANTITHESIS: The ultimagte standard for care is its cost-effectiveness. The 20-pound Pelosi bil does not define what cost-effective is. That will be left up to the Washngton bureaucrats who will rule on the material ie. money value of your lives. The socialist scorn for compassionate and competent doctors will soon become apparent. The Hyppocraic oath "do no harm"

will translate into "how much is this man's care worth to the State?" That solution is fraudulent and evil.

THESIS: There will be no healthcare provided for illegal aliens.
ANTITHESIS: Illegals need only hide or falsify their identity to avail themselves of Nationalized healh care. Take that to the bank. The governemt will know your bank balance anyway to determine if you have chated the buraucrats.

THESIS: There will be no care for abortion on demand.
ANTITHESIS: Subborned racketeer Doctors will falsify the patient needs of the pregnant woman. Fewer than 1% now qualify—e.g.rape, incest, DAB . . . .

THESIS: Tort reform is built into the new system, by way of the Secretary's (Commissioner's) board of advisory doctors in Washington.
ANTITHESIS: I laugh at your hypocrisy. The monster bill allows more loopholes for Obama's lawyer suppoters, fraud of kickbacks and bribes and corruption of existing laws, extravagant legal fees, corrupt paybacks, rotten malpratilce by attorneys—all these deviations from hnesty in contracts and relationships will sap taxpayer money by the hundreds of billions of dollars. You can take that to the bank.

The bill has passed the Senate. Meantime, you crooks and fool Democrats in the House have your care. You will attempt to "fix" the Senate bill by individual reconciliation. a bill the Senate's fixeswhich you have neither seen nor voted upon. Then you will, having passed your version of Obamacare, give a "deemed" voted upon, the Senate bill as a pass, At that point, trickly Pelosi's hands will be separated from the two bills, and zend the Horrible Senate bill to Obama to sign.

The bill now law, will lack the reconciliation fixes, however. It will lack the passage by the House vote. It will be un-Constitutional. The President will be engaging in a criminal act, a flagrant violati of Article I, Section 7 of the US constitution which requires that both Houses vote on the sametext, not one an Obama care text and the other a Reconciliation Text. You have been duluded by false prophets. God's curse upon your evil design that interdicts the true inter-personal healing of dedicated health professionals. The bill is anti-human, political throughout and sub-human,; for it allows no tolerance for the working wisdom of true humanitarian health care. Like Obama's aiy speeches, he will greet the nation with cheers, supercilious without any real substance of effective care.

ADDENDUM:

NOTE: the AMA represents only 17% of the doctors and they are students, interns, reirees, doctors working in a proteced enfirnment such as Universities. The Other 88% are not members. The joining of the AMA to Obamacare was soleldy a decision of the leadership to retain their 75 million dollar franchise with the government that entitles them to represent America.
President Obama said you can keep your doctors—that is a lie
President Obama said you can keep your present insurance policy—that is a lie.
President Obama said you you will not pay for illegal aliens—that is a lie in the absence of specific prohibitions.
President Obama said you will not pay more for health insurance—that is a lie

The entire Sunday night vote by the House to pass the "reconcilition"—fixes Bill will be a fraud against the American people. Done—at midnight, the doors locked, the media prohibited. That procedure will be fraudulent, deceptive, dishonest, misleading, shameful and a disgrace to the entire Congress before the eyes of the world and before our next generations. The doctors are now standing tall. They realize that they will not be able to give adequagte, skilled and professional care to their patients under Obamacare. One lie would be enough to disqulify a President's credibility. But four lies!-and this is just about health care.

The Senate bill will bring about bureaucratic muddling in patient care, sepaation of patient and doctor, great quantieies of mistakes in transmission, breakdowns in electronic communication, distant life-threatening dexcisions, no toleance for changes in patient conditions, post opeative crises, traumatic injuries that require instant attention, misdiagnoses from a distance. The Stae wil beyour consdience.

There will be shortages in doctors, nurses, attendant personnel, LPN's, PN's, technicians. There will come shortages of critical drugs, shortages in down-sized hospitals, shortages in beds, shutdowns of entire wards, rampant occupation by illegal aliens. There will come mistakes in identification of patients, descriptions of medical problems, mistakes in diagnoses and surgeries, mixups in names, crucial reverses of treatment, the reappearance of long-ago conquered diseases such as Tuberculosis an diptheria. The way is wide open for fraud in drug dispensing, costs for operation surgeries. Trial lawsyers like sharks will circle hospitals waiting for disgruntled patients to file suit. Even interuption of medical communication can cost a life. What about a week to repair facilities interupted for some unforsen cause. On and On. Obamacvare simply will not work work. Within the first year, you will see the light and regret your foolish decision, Leftists and hardshell liberals in both houses of Congress will witness with dismay the collapse of Obamacare . . .

To "completely transform America" is Obama;s stated reason as to why he got into politics. To transform is to change so remarkably and completely that the previous forms of government, laws, conditions, character and Constitution no longer exist, except perhaps in memory and by empty salutation. His intentions are evil,—ev en though some see himas a nice-guy whose liberal philosopjhy led him to make bad choices and mistakes! The Senate billl having never been voted upon but only deemed passed is not valid law, except as the dictator Obama declares it to be so. We are now living in a nascent, forming-up and viable dictatorship of one man and his Oligarchy of Socialist-Democrat supporters in the government. He has the suppor of a prostituted media. The unwashed masses no longer count. The serfs are made ready to do his bidding. At present he is his own Minister of Propaganda. We are waiting for the President to appoint his Czar of Information (propaganda).

REFORM AMERICA,
CENSURE HER FRIENDS,
FLATTER HER ENEMIES

The gang of pirates from Obama on down through Greasy Axelrod, Rahm 1 & 2, Sanctus Sanctorum Pelosi, Bendable Reid, Treasury Feinstein, Tenth-Round Boxer, More Light, Waxman, Cash Stentosis Geitner, All's Well Napolitano, Eric (the bull) Holder, Cyclist Kerry, Barnacle Frank, Cris-cross Dodd, Swastica Durbin, Frog—in—is-Throat Leahy . . . this gang of looped up radical detestables is determined to trash American history and the most human, inventive and deployable system in medical care ever known to Western civilization. In its place these Lilliputians will substitute the pathetic, impractical, clumsy and corrupt system invented by a social outcast, Karl Marx in a London Library. Now it's up to the people to clean up Freedom Street.

The Obamacare plan lacks Constitutional restraints, oversight, is subject to manpulation for fraud that rips off the taxpayers, fattens the trial lawyers and that will lead our medical care to mediocrity, incompetence, ongoing lawsuits, massive confusion of data, mistakes in judgement and partial care, and virtual total destruction, of a working healthcare that will become totally inadquate, as in "advanced" Europe.

Do you admire European medicine? Go there for your heart surgery. You may die first. It is sad, is it not, that our State Department Head Hillary Clinton cherishes Marx's memory! Marxism is weak, inadequate, impractical, fraudulent and wrong for free men, if not for European Medieal serfdom. Give one example of its success in "advanced" (Obama) Western history.

You want to be a Swede or a Dane? Go. You'll wait two years for a total hip replacement, and then it may be inferior. You accept our President's lie, do you not? These pirates and other leftists—Socialist-Democrats—and hard-shelled liberals in the Congress—including the free-radicals called Tsarists—Olinsky-inspired bureaucrats wallowing in un-Constitutional power—working with the leftist administration are going to destroy this great nation by their adamant, unforgiving, desperate, wicked will, by which phrase Churchhill described Hitler. Already, Obama's backup will be cadres of Highschoolers trained to condemn capitalism, border security, industrialization, and citizenship status in the US. To secure his next term in office, Obama is inviting illegals to cross our borders, who at a proper time will be declared legals—given Biodata cards like the rest of us—and beneficiaries of Obamacare. They will constitute a 10-million voting lock for his next term in office, if and when Amnesty arrives. You may absolutely count on that!! If you need open heart surgery and can get it after 18 months, you may have to dump out of bed an illegal alien bedded down for leg cramps while picking lettuce—if the Socialist-Democrat Federal Government will permit you to do so.

These and other political degenerates are determined to install Obmacare by the devious trickery of reconciliation vote (originally for monetary bills), that will install the Senate version (as a rider) after the "deemed," the presumed, passage of the signed Senate version. And we, the people, do not see this ungrateful cheat on our will, our labor, our vision, our history? Tell me I successfully attended and graduated from Hollywod High, UCLA, Stanford U. I am an intelligent man. How can a bill not voted upon by the House—count beome the law of the land, Constitutionally? It cannot. It is a paper law, a "law" insubstance only, not in application. Unless, unless, a tyrant declares it to be a law without Constiltutional process. NOTE:—Obama's raillery at "process." Now you see why he rebuked conservatives for their emphasis on "due process." The "deemed" vote by the House on a major piece of legislation is a mere "process." Do you dumbed-down journalists get it? I'm sure you do and you find that Obama's end justifies the means of silence.

Without morals or ethics, these scavenges on democratic ideology will crow. "At last we got Healthcare for all!"—translated meaning—State control of not one but all major industries in the US, the Marxist state, the debt 1.3 trillions of taxpayer dollars. And yet you are so frigin stupid you do not see why people are out of work and have no cnsumer money to spend! You s . . . heads in power are a joke when it comes to brains; since even common sense carries a simple warning of catastrophe. Money? What is that to the leftists? Ours becomes theirs to spend without responsible control or ethical conscience. Selah! We will get used to the tyranny, they say . . . like the frog in a pot of hot water that slowly heats up undetected by the frog that never jumps out before it is cooked.

Leaders? You would lead us down the "road to serfdom," you you empty-minded fatheads wthout a pot to render you in, your wisdom, and heartless chests swollen with illusury beneficince. You would make us servants to the government based on a failed European ideology that you somehow find acquaintance with and compatability with. I suspect it is convenient for your careers to do so. What colossal selfishness and the greed of Me-ism. You are delusional and drunk with power, all of you, the Prelates of Govement and the quibbling Scions of Journalism. That includes the President—in your faces you followers of Rules for Radicals. instead of the US Constitution.

Where does it say: "The Congress shall represent a suitable ideology intead of the will of the people?

All new offices (Tsars) established by the Executive shall not represent the people, but rather delude the people in secret in order to promote the prosperity of all. You're politically sick. Equality of virtue, talent, ambition and achievement is the product of tyranny. Making it so is the sword of power. Because you think Marxism will work in its coat of fashion called "Fascism" you would impose on the American people, by guile, deceptiona and lies, instituted and led by Barack Obama, a regime alien to our history, repugnant to our people's will and destructive of our glorious history and the intentions of our Founding Fathers. Who in hell do you think you are, since you speak from hell, the hell of tyranny and not from the capacious space of risk, opportunity and rewards and liberty? Elected to be leaders, you would become our tyrant overlords, regardless of our rejection of your corrupt regime-plans. His Majesty Obama calls that "hope."

The Obamacare is in actualtiy a death-wish for America. It is an insult to our collective intellience as a people. It is a purgation of common sense and a ridicule of the God, whom he never mentions, who gave us our fundamental rights, not the State you would create and have us to worship. America is wealthy because for over two hundred yrs we have invented, developed, invested in our ideas and projects and exploited our naturalr esources to bring this great nation to the position of exceptional wealth and visible production with God's help and our own initiative. You forget that America was an isolationist nation before Pearl Harbor awakened the giant. At this point in our history, we do not want Obama;s fraudulent leadership. He sat in Wright's church for 20 years trying credibly to justify his distrustful hatred for America, AS IT IS by changing it to align with mentor Saul Olinsky's Rules for Radials in your Chicago community. Those "Rules For Radicals"?

RULE # 1: The wealth of America has been accumulated at the expense of the rest of the world. If you gain a position of power apoligize to the billions of poor ripped off, exploited by American capitalists.

But I tell you, Mister President, You never worked and sweated a day of your life at a skilled trade, day labor job, a business ownership. You're an elitist fraud who is above such common pursuits in life. When you promise to create more jobs, you don't know what the hell you are talking about, Barack Hussein—America is wealthy not "at the expense of the rest of the world but because of he above virtues of enterprise, investment and hard work, as I say, in isolation largely unitl WW II. The rest of the world was so undevelopd that the impoverilshed peoples had nothing they could use or afford made in the United States. We had all the coal, timber, factories, labor we needed. for ourselves. Rip offs . . . ? America as exploiter of the world? That;s the slosh from some brain-dead liberal Havard professor.

RULE #2. Reverse the process by returning America's wealth to the poor and starving peoples of the rest of the world. (I have never heard mention of Appalachia!) Begin in America by massive taxation to make the exploiters the "greedy corporations" and private investors, i.e. Wall Street capitialists know how it feels to be robbed of their wealth—your colossal Marxlist lie. Do so with dignity, statutory trickery, authenticity and calm. Let lies and bribery be two of your best tools. The ruck of the American people is too stupid to see through your Humnanist schemes. That is your delusion. They are a smug, presumptuous lot about their history. Ignore it. Ignore them.

RULE #3. Since Capitalist wealth was stolen by deception, deception is the name of the game you must play, behind locked doors when necessary. Do not listen to their appeals of simple-minded honesty. They are hypocrites; you are always—apology—almost always right.

RULE #4: Never admit that you are wrong, under any circumstances. That will only weaken your offense against monsterous capitalist greed. You must, however, be ruthless with the changes or enlightened socialism will not work. You are the bringer of new life to America. However, Barack, you do not have the foggest notion of what competition is. All of your bailouts are free-throws from the foul line of unlawful encroachment called CEO firings and contractual re-arrangements. An anarchist, you are a law unto yourself, Mister Obama.

RULE # 5: Mollify the discontents, for they lack the intelligence to discern your vision, or to appreciate all that can be done for them by your government. You can mollify them by small trade-offs, careful use of the word "jobs" to signify increases, and subtle expressions of sympathetic contenpt for the America AS IT IS which has brought so much misery to the rest of the world. I will act with one swift blow . . . we will pass this bill by Easter (hallelujah, the risen Christ), a bill the American people are "entitled to." Utilize all other such expressions that betray cynicism and disdain for our capitalist, democratic, free-market, entrepreneur system of government and ways of life. If this bill passes, the people will not for a long time have good faith and confidence in their elected representatives, if they betray the people by voting YES for Obamacare. Those who vote YES and live through the next decade will be filled with remorse, but as Johnthan Edwards admonished the non-believers in his congregation one Sunday morning, "Too late! too late sinner . . . beyond the reach of the love of God!"

To the above names and all other leftists and hard-core liberals who push for bigger and bigger government through Obama's agenda programs, I tell you—you godless souls are not worth the cost of Normandy's Omaha beach. You abuse your power to realiize a defunct, speculative and corrupting ideology. You will make the selfishness of massive entitlements a virtue. You will, in doing so, feel that your are protected by the perfect justice of the socialist State, the "virtuous" state.

See the fields of little white crosses above the cliffs at Normandy? Some drowned, some were shot, some lay in agony with wounds from mortars, mines, some were maimed, some survived to fight . . . . but none ever, ever gave up fighting to the last because they were and we are Americans. We don't want your God-damned European lifestyle of total dependence upon the government, Obama et al! Okay? Let those words be in your faces! Find our names on the WW II memorial in Washsington, DC.

I pray that God will damn your plan to rip America out of honst history by the roots in order to glorify your image, Mister President and your leftist cohorts. See if God approves of the "trick" Madam Pelosi—the swaggerstick, spendthrift Pelosi—spoke of. Semi-illiterate that she is, she borrowed the word from Sen. Reid who, as a kid, swam in a cathouse pool. He knows something about the larger deception of a marital "trick"

When it comes to warfare, homeland security and protection . . . and to economics and medicine for 300,000,000 people, most of you lifeless, spoiled-rotten freaks of elitist perpetuity don't know shit from Shinola. But you are determined to please His Majesty and his radical Rump Parliament. Maybe I should pray for you, because you will assuredly displease the God of creation, source of wisdom for a city on a hill, one of a kind in human history, a threat to tyrants, a blessing to the suffering, a rock for the exile and a champion of justice. Our strengths are not good enough for you. Your mindset is to trash traditions, Constituional powers when expedient, vitality of innovation, compassion in the character America that I know is, to my enlightened mind, incomprehensible.

You are a President of expediency. Therefore, the rush to pass your bill. You. the me-generation, are a generation that lacks character. Go ahead. You've got to see to believe. Throw away 21st century America by your simple-minded, selfish concentration of power in Washington. You'll never, ever get her back. There will (probably) be no repeal of your impotent bill, whatever the version! But you will be famous in hisory. That is what you really want, Mister Obama, President of the United States—to be famous in history regardless of the will of the people!

Bipartisanship, to you, Mister President, is achieved by the use of force to gain unity, and by force I mean:-

1—seizure of whole industries, auto, banking, energy, media, education . . .

2—over-regulation that destroys competition, profit from competition is alien to the Govenment you envison, the marxist Stae.

3—dishonest manipulation of statutory law, i.e First Amendment

4—trash-disposal of Constitutional restraints,

5—corruption of the Congress with your money,

6—healthcare rationing, no death panel but shortages, shortages due to removal of ugly profit,

7—bribery of an entire state by the promise of free health care "forever,]'

8—secret locked committee sessions,

9—a White House dinner to bribe the recalcitrant Senators,

10—the use of financial reconciliation as a tactic to pass 9 pounds of confusing legislation, a bill of entangled crap!

11—attempted control of the media by electronic incitements, pressure on media unions (supporters)

12—encouragement of political snitches!!

13—lies (# 1: not everybody can get emergency medical care and or timely medical intervention

14—broken promises, broken promises!! (Promise # 1: you can keep your own doctor. Ohhh? Tell me, master)—all threats to our every-day lives, to say the least.

15—crushing taxation. (See: sale of nationlal assets to raise funds for a bankrupt nation. The envious nations can hardly wait. I-10, becomes across-country toll road for Gemany's enrichment; The national parks bercome Spanish property. Bankrupt Amtrack becomes the property of a Japanese consortium . . . . How do you like that, you tax and—spend lefilst scum in the Congress? Hmmm? You'd like to have at me. Line up.

16—delusionl job creation by the Federal government. When you tax to raise money to spend to "create" jobs, you destroy the base for the true creation by business when you remove their capacity to hire workers in the irst place. because you scorn profit from which those workers are paid. Dummu!. That truth escaps you as the bla, bla, bla of more bailouts deepens the national debt and creates only the illusion of progress. The fiends of hell worked of that ditty about "progressive government."

The stench of socialist mismanagement and oppressive regulation, insane taxation, wanton irresponsible spending is smellable way out here on the West Coast.

Vocal, democratic resistance is called "obstructionism." While you have silenced the mainstream media by the prostitution of their unions, and have enjoyed your jamboree with supportive public employee unions (includes UTLAU) and have bought off fence-sitters, you continue to plead a causus belli against middle-class America. You're a case all right of dishonest Chicago-barrio politics consortium of radical liberals and Lefists. The mobsters could not have done a better job of pauyoff politics.

Pontius Pilate asked the crowd with derision, "What is truth?" with reference to "criminal" Christ's teachings. Truth to Pilate was the sword. The Truth to you, Mister President, is the sword of Federal power used to abuse the people—by intimidation and fiscal exhaustion—into compliance with a foreign doctrine and theory of governmen that has never worked, ever, ever. Instead of blood, the surrender of our freedoms to taxation and Federal control of our entire lives will cause to perish the gleaming battlement and holy offerings of suffrance we are able, thus far, to extend to the rest of the world. Where in Western History has the United Srates ever approached the rest of the world to beg, to capture, to enslave, to exploit and rapaciously to impoverish? I eschew your scumbag lie, purloined by your egregious professors at Harvard.

Your sword of Federal power will extinguish the light of liberty forever in this great nation. Not we or our children, or their children for genrations to come will ever forgive you misguided, nepotists, sychophantic, blood suckers, thieves because you would steal away the heart of this nation. The words of those who love this country will not go unanswered or ignored by future generaions when they see how we stood in the breech to fight you parasites on liberty. Can you say you love your wife if you send her out onto street to whore for you . . . because a putah named Alinsky prescribes the action for an ideology, the ideology of tyrants, as total submission to the State?

SOCIALISM,
A FAILED STATIST THEORY

Two principles of life inspired our Founders:

(1) Man is imperfect, he is fallible and makes mistakes and commits crimes against the people; and

(2) He has a sin-nature which he cannot avoid but is compelled to use to his selfish advantage, such as to seize, control and feel the exhilaration of power over others. President Obama is a version of Captain Ahab of Melville's PEQUOD, who, against the reason of his First Mate, destroyes his ship and his crew—except for the cabn boy—by attempting to avenge his missing leg, bitten off by MOBY DICK, the monster beast (Socialism) a great albino right whale that, maddened by the chase, smashes into the ship, sinks it and drowns the innocent seamen. That is what socialism will do to America, destroy her, like the Pequod. We have the similar madness, an ideological, desperate madness among the leftists in control of the ship of state called REPUBLIC. They are working against reason. They will cost us trillions of dollars before they are retired . . . to the status of lobbyists!

There were three principles that led to the Constitutional Congress' document of the separation of powers in government, (a) to execute, (b) to judge, (c) to create. The Founders understood the abuses of power. They created a three-branch government to avoid the concentration of power. They spelled-out the restraints on each branch, prescribed for the citizens and intended to be read by them. The sections that over the three branches contain a clear enumeration of the citizens' rights that are to remain protected and inviolable for so long as the nation shall exist. From the President on down, our present one-party d;emocrat government yearns to abolish the God-given rights and that definitive separation of the three branches of powers, together with the specilic protections of citizen rights from encroachments by that government. President Obama would prompt the people to believe that the Constitution is too much a document about what the government cannot do rather than what it can do. That is a lie; he supposes that Americans are illiterate European peons, third-world subjects of a ruling power, his rule, his power. Without those proective constraints on the three branches of our government, tyranny arrises, inevitably . . . as it has already . . . a national socialism imitative of socialism in Germany called "Nazism." You poliical deviates make the change sound so "innocent" and "right" and "democratic" and "compassionate." All those assumtions are lies.

There's nothing wrong with national bankruptcy, except impoverishment of the people—the REPUBLIC crashed and sunk by the great albino whale named SOCIALISM. When our National debt exceeds our GNP, our Gross National Production, we can sell the national Cathedral, the US Park System, Mount Rushmore, toll roads declared so throughout the US, (the NAFTA superhighway I-35 already has a Spanish checkpoint in Kansas!) airports and facilities, harbors and facilities . . . these precious possessions to be auctioned off on the world market to make up the deficit of the present and past administrations, creators of the national debt of 14 trillions of dollars that will continue to burden our succesors for decades. Sold out! Assets, revenue makers, precious properties . . . . The Presdent projects before the world and the UN a New World Order, for which the United States is to be the sacrificial lamb. To redistribute our wealth, the President will need, nay, will fabicate policies to reconstruct a socialist society by the imposiltion of 50% taxation on each middle-class citizen—an income tax to pay off the entitlements not just of Americans but of the world!

He will attempt to install cradle-to-grave oversight? . . . yes. That is his "vision" for America, not by derelection of duty but by ideological intention of design. That is a succinct depiction of Obama's oligarchial utopian fantasy. "The people will get the government they deserve." Jefferson sald. We have a Repulic, if we can keep it, Franklyn said. The people will get the governent they need—Obama says. The people will get the country they struggle for—Washington would have said. The present Administration, therefore, is attempting to destroy the very foundations of our society as a people, as a nation. Period. To those determined to overthrow the will of the American people, I say, when we throw you contemptible Leftists out of office, go to Europe where you belong. You will be happier there. Socialism is all set up and ready to go for you. We conservatives can arrange a Cruise Ship—an investment of capital—to ferry your soulless corpses to the Utopia of European socialism. So long, champions of Marxism! You jerks need to be micromanaged by a European government. Certainly the people who are too stupid to understand your Marxist propaganda cannot affect your decisions there.

I'm a publihed Author. Years ago Univesity Editions, a West Virginia company now out of busness, published a book of mine entitled DIARY OF A PRISONER (1958). My dedication is to—"All patriots who protested the power of America's bureaucratic Central Government to invade the lives of is citizens, since they believed that such intimate intrusions and the consequenve of punishment and death abrogated their inalienable rights, blasphemed a Holy God and destroyed their precious Liberty, these offenses giving them just cause to revolt."

More significant and surprising this day to me is what I wrote on the cover those fifty years ago. Keep in mind that the central character in my book was "caught" reading seditious literature, such as the Bible, on public property. The US Constitution, flamatory essays by Paine and Jeffeson, treatises on liberty . . . done on public property, in this case in a public park instead of in a private home, activated the thought police to enforce Political Correctness. Already God is irrelevant in Amercan schools, declared to be so by men in black robes. The guilty seditionist in my book was thrown into an internment camp for political and social dissenters, expecially set up within barbed wire for those who opposed the State's power to control the intimate concerns, choices, options, indeed the lives of all the people . . . . all 300,000,000 of us. Does that not smack of evil and insanity?

We may have arrived. Observe! This introduction appeaed on the cover of the same book: "My sorrow is profound as I look back into history and see as a witness, nay as a survivor amid the rubble, the death of a once-glorious nation, America. They had forgotten their God, their Christian heritage, the motivating wisdom of their forefathers and the anguish of the struggle required to give birth to the freedoms their leaders corrupted and the people looked upon with ingratitude and indifference. I was there yet escaped to tell others of the horrors of unbridled anarchy and satanic seizure in one of nuimerous prison camps for remnant dissenters against tyranny. I am not a prophet but I understand the evil inherent in injustice and the Logic of Ultimaacy. The faith of our forefathers was not the anathema but the remedy. Reason had made of man his own icon. With it he could play with the universe, being thus accountable only to himself."

We are today, a half-century later, even closer to that catastrophe of the destruction of our glorious United States of America, "sweet land of liberty, of thee we sing . . . ."

"We are standing on the threshhold of history," all right, Madam Speaker, the history of the trashing of Americxa by you and your liberal and leftist ilk in the Congress and in the administration. You have to be certifiably stupid, all of you, not to see and appreciate unspeakable wisdom of our nation's founders, embedded in our historic documents. The socialists in Washngton will have to purge our history by delectable substitutions of pop stars for historic leaders and corrupti the the language of liberty in order to demean her as a way of life . . . likened to Europeans.

Recenly Speaker Pelosi uttered these words: "We must pass this bill in order to know what it says." Rattle the bill, people, and guess what's inside. That is leadership? That is an unconscionbly unlawful invitation . . . indicating that the House still does not know what the bill contains. Surprise! You will, instead, attempt by your vote on Obamacare to "rebuild" America, whatever that means. It means what that 9-pound bill of tangled, legalese nonsense means when the government interprets it for us recipients of its "largesse." Your pompous, arrogant, narcissistic and ill-informed course is to destroy historic America and substitute a European State instead. May the God of our Founders help us!

Here is a short list of countries that have tried the system you hope in your abyssmal ignorance to make us accept . . . a system that has never worked, even at the muzzle of a gun—socialilsm or, inanother word, Statism, tyranny, dictatorship. Tyranny grants no middle ground to the people.

1—Joseph Stalin, the Soviet Union. He murdered 30 millions of the peoples of Russia and the Soviet satellites to get his way.

2—Pot Pol, Kmuhr Rouge. He murdered one fourth of his own people to get his way.

3—Adolph Hitler, Germany under the national Socialist German Workers Party (the Nazis). He murdered 600,000 Jews to "cleanse" Germany and brought about the deaths of 150 millions more to get his own way

4—Leonid Breshnev, Soviet Union. He statism was brought down by President Ronald Regan as a worthless system of government behind "that wall," a government that had opted to control the globe through the UN

5—Fidel Castro, Cuba. He murdered at least 50,000 of his own people. No wonder Cubans flee in rowboats to reach the US! And he calls Obamacare passage a "miracle."

6—Kim Il Sung, North Korea. He is favorite of Lady Clintonn . . . in our government, depite the loss of some 50.000 American lives in the "forgotten war."

7—Tito, Yugoslavia. The figures are untold, he shot dissenters, as those tyrants always do, for lack of compliance. How do you expect to enforce compliance in Amerca, you lilly-livered chicken-brained Leftist escapees from an insane asylum? Hmmme? Threaten to take our homes by taxes, by sheriff's possee deputized as Federal Agents and wihout cause or Court warrant. We are armed—the wisdom in the 2nd amendment!

8—Ho Chi Minh, Vitetnam. There are 56.000 warrior names engraved on that black obsidion wall in Washington, DC. Defended. loved, sacrificed to secure this nation's freedom and freedom around the world. To you, they are worthless, the wall is simply a fixture for visitors to see, the flowers, cards, notes of loved ones. But no, you prefer the country they fought against to be adopted by us in the "reform" you would impose on the American people. Go to the wall, obseve the flags and "lifted" names of the sacrifices and tell the people, by your vote, they wasted their lives by fighting a system and tyranny of life now deemed to be a perfectly useable system of Statist control in America. Shout it out, you Leftist swine, that these momuments, including that for WW II veterans, were ventures in wrong-headed futility and the dismal failure of Republican democracy. Tell the world your lie—that Obamacare is democratic.

9—Huey P. Long, communist—"leaning" governor of Louisiana in the 1930's. It was "famous for removing opposition."

Extol these dictators, you excuses for leaders, frauds upon the story of this nation. There is Venezuelan Caesar Chaves, buddy buddy of Obama. There is a benign statism in Canada, Great Britain and "advanced" nations like Denmark, Sweden and Norway. Obama becomes our king, like theirs, does he not? We will dump your shining emoluments on the pavement come election time. Count on it. We know who you are We the people are now informed. But go ahead, "Transform" America. by imposing on her a monstrous foreign ideology. Remember one thing, greedy muckers for power-control over the American people, in order for the socialist system to work, Socialism must (1) be enforced by intimidation and death into compliance by all the people at one time, not piecemeal, therefore (2) all the parts must work similtaneously or it falls apart. No more independent decisons by inividuals involved in their medical care, no more close relationships and trust between doctors and patients, no more taking of risks to find new pharmaceutals and invent healhcare machines, devices . . . because the virtuouis state defines profit as bad and "unfair," thereby killing the people's trust in health care in their country

You cannot have it both ways. Either total control or haphazard innovation. You have yet to see the mess you will create, an oxymoron. In your Leftist arrogance you will not be able to withstand the latter. You think the electronic transcription of details for 900 million businesses, small and large into a computer data base in the US will prove effective, by whose authority?—the word of some whoremonger bureaucrat in Washington DC office? This is life or death for America! Obmaare is a death wish for this great nation and for a medical care system that has worked as no other since the deveopment of Western civilization . . . to replace the Medieval s barbarisms you prefer. Blood-letting by leeches to cure a disease or abate a fever . . . . "advacd" European medicine. Even Geman medicine lags behind American technology and medical intelligence. ILt's because of our medical schools and our profit-making innovative practices, stupid!

You want to get rid old people becaue they are not worth the cost of their care, as in China, that mandates the aborttion of a kind, a gender, an entire generation in order to increase their (your) army of State-pleasers. You will have us to support abortion with our money, and in other areas of medicine ration what we are presently capable of treating, etc. Try us. I spit in your collecive faces, Leftist bureaucrats. We conservatives are at war wih you, and war is nasty, ugly, cruel, bloody and incompehensble to the appeasers. That includes that fraud of an American in the White House. You have not yet heard him rage against this country if Obamacare should fail. You do not know the man altlhough you think you do. We are "endowed by our Creator with cetain inalienable rights, that among these are Life, Liberty and the pursuit of Happiness."

NOTE for Leftist Usurpers: The State does not make men equal. God has created them to be equal before Him. The State forces men to appear to be equl by compliance with standards of conformity and uniformity. Their unique qualities as individuals remain hidden, the agens of rebellion and revolution. We, therefore, have an outlaw administration in power whose leader is obsessed with "completely transforming America." That agenda by any other name is outlawry by the President. Yet because we are a people of laws and not of violence, we will have to throw the pirates overboard at the next election. May they drown in their sea of incipient violence and self-love.

OBAMA DICTATORSHIP
OVER AMERICA

I present a declaration of Federal intent, process and ultimate results:

1) Obamacare is largely a tax-revenue bill to expunge private insurers, enrich the government, extend politician tenure of office and exert control over the people by its seizure of the free market, the President having already seized the auto and banking industries with the intent to seize education viz a viz centralized loans for students. All tax bills must originate in the House. Obamacare originated in the Senate.

Art i, Sec. 7: "All Bills for raisng Revenue shall originate in the House of Repesentatives; but the Senate may propose or concur with Amendments as on other Bills." It is an deception of the people by the President and the Congress for them to to assert that Obamacare is not designed to redistribute the wealth of the people of America, howsoever the means is described in the Senate bill. When abilll involvs one-sixth of the American economy, it is more than a bill of attainder.

2) A bill that originates in either House must pass in the identical text to the other House. The House of Representatives on Sunday voted to pass the reconciliation bill instead of the Obamacare bill. When it was declared, deceptively, by Speaker Nancy Pelosi that the bill "is passed", she expected the people to assume that it was the Senate Obamacare bill, whereas, in truth, it was the bill of particulars in the Reconciliation "package" bill that had passed. She imputed passage of the Senate bill when she said "the bill has been" 'deemed' i.e (assumed) passed. What in fact had passed

was the Reconciliation bill with its "fixes." This is unacceptable for major leglislation.

3) At this juncture in the process—process having been condemned by Obama as unnecessary and irrrelevan, divisive (we now see why), the Senate bill was "deemed," assumed, to have passed in the House. That is a breech of oath by the House members and constitutes fraud against the American people. There is no provision in Article I of the Constitution to grant legal legitimacy and authority to a major piece of legislation that has not been read, comprehended, adjudicated by and handed over to the other House. In no place in the US Constitution is it warranted, accepted or condoned that a text different from the original text be substituted for that original, as has occurred in this case.

4) A bill must pass by means of a vote by the lower House of Representatives. It cannot be assumed, deemed, to have passed without that vote. Obamacare "passed" to the lower house as an assumed, a deemed-to-have-passed bill. An assumption involves a judgement. Tha judemen will be challenged by individual States.

5) The Senate bill was never voted on by the Houe of Representatives as was evdenced by the trickery of Reconciliation yet President Obama declared the fraudulent Senate-only bill to be Law. Both the Obamacare bill and the President's signed declaration are fraudulent and illegal by virtue of their procedual irregularity. What we have instead of a lawful piece of legislaion is a law in substance on paper yet impossible, wirhout coercive unlawful interventionl by the Government in people's lives, an edict by the State, a command that is tyranny on its face as well as in its intent and substance.

6) The provision that the government can command a citizen to purchase an insurance product is unlawful. The government does not and cannot show that to be an enumerated power and therefore presentation of that provision, its implementation, including fines and imprisonment, are unlawful. They constitute abuses of Federal power and an endanerment to the continued existence of our free society.

To charcterize the Feeral government as acting in a lawful way when the above policy propositions are deemed to be valid charges is an abuse of power, a seizure of power, a mischaracterization of the people's government and their representatives and a duplicitous act that endangers the freedoms of this nation, not the least of which is Amendment X of the US Constitution. I quote:

AMENDMENT X—"The powers not delegated to the United States by the Constituion, nor prohibited by it to the States, are reserved to the States respectively or to the people." Each State posesses the Constitutional right to block Obamacare.

Conclusion: Neither the power to override either House by President's final mandate, nor the power to suppose, characterize and implement a bill not properly and lawfully passed by both houses with amendments is a shortcut, an abridgement of the Constitution that by its purpose, announcement and implementation is unlawful

For the President to sign a bill that has not passed by a simple majority of both houses is a fraudulent cheat upon the people, depriving them of the benefit of lawful legislation by way of an unlawful bill which they must accept and perform under, although on its face it is fraudulent. The bill known as Obamacare is therefore an outlaw piece of legislation and deserves both to be challenged in the court for its entirety, as well as for certain provisions orderilng that citizens purchase a product. It deserves to be discarded as the illegal usurpation of power by the President. He has signed a bill that embraces his persosnal agenda, as well as that of his oligarchical officials both in the Congress and in his administration.

This bill, I surmise and believe, is but the prelude to the enlargement of the Federal Government to such an extent that the will of the people, expunged in this instance, is no longer a valid test of our democratic process of representative government but, instead, is the instigation and beginning of a political dictatorship.

Remember that Obama has promised to "completely transform America." Transform means to change to such a degree and extent and in such ways that the original character of America is no longer discernable to the people who live therein. That intention is an announcement of the intent by this administraiton, which is to enlarge government to the extent, degree and size that representative government no longer exists and the offices of the administration need no longer be filled by people who represent, reflect and embody the will of the American people. Voing booths will become, thereupon, mere symbols of what is no longer effective democratic, representative government. A single party in support of a dictator always wins at the polls. The trickery I have described above is not a "misdemeanor," a Constitutional check upon Presidenial abuse of power. The trickery exercised in the Congress defies the will of the people, for whom this nation was founded and for the protection of whom our Founding Fathers designed the US Constitution. The reach of Obamas's tyranny will only grow as his admnisration enlarges the Federal Government to the size of an omnipotent oligarchy that makes of the individual a nonentity and the citizen a mere slave in its ruthless seizure of power.

KING GEORGE COPYCAT

The President who compares his sleeqy spendthrift program for the last 9 months with the cause and character of our history is a charlatan, a liar to the world, an appeaser to their envy and a blidn guide to the naive and unlearned. Is his performance the equal in character and merit to our wars to free the peoples of the world, our compassion after in calamities worldwide, our hardy growth from New England colonies, through the Cumberland Gap westward to the Pacific ocean, our mighty developments of industry at the turn of the 19th centujry and our dependence from our founding documents to the present upon an omnipotent God, source and guaranto of our lilfe, liberty and the pursuit of happiness.

Instead, let me cite from the Declaration of Independence the transgressions upon our history by the Obama program, become visible these last nine months. He proclaimed at his recent UN Speech that he was the "king of kings," ururping Christ's place in the context of Holy Scripture.

Let us state the rulings (we know not all his Executive Orders) that dismay a noble and great people.

1) "He has erected a multitude of offices, and sent/appointed Swarms of Officers to harrass our People and eat out their Substance. (expansion of present DC agencies and surrounding Officers of His Administration that includes Tsars and every conceivable mode for the exercise of political power by his adminstration. He has failed consistently to submit his Executive Orders to the Congress for their approval, but, instead, has ordered that they be executed wthout pause or query. The silent media have been complicit in this mode of Presidential secrecy, a fact that augers ill for this nation of freedom. A tyrant who acts in secret and without the consent of the body

that represents the will of the people acts corruptly, both out of the will of God and out of the law of the land. The Health Care, the Cap and Tax are but starters, for he has pass the one with duplicitous maneuvering between the Houses, and it can be expected that he will coerce into law the latter in the same manner, deceitfully without a hand-count/.

2) He has kept among us in times of peace, standing Army withoutt he Conent of our Legislatures. (FEMA) He has proposed, initillyby suggestion only, an INS, National security force "as well trained and as well funded as the military." This can be taken to mean a national police force, as in Europe which will be, or can be, activated by meana of the Biodata card that all citizens will be ordered to carry.

3) He has affected (coming) to render the Military independent and superior to the Civil Power. (His National Security forces to come, as well-fundecd as the militarty).)

4) He has combined with others to subject us to a jurisdition foreign to our Constitution and unacknowledged by our Laws, giving his Assent to their Acts of pretended Legislation. (Appeals by justices, his appintees, of our Supreme Courtthat accept or eliminate foreign rulings by the Hague Court of three judges in Amsterdam) He has encouraged an openness by liberal SC judges to sharia law, "where practical," President Obama has encouraged legislation from the bench by thesilmple expedient of acknowledging the xperience of his appointees—not their knowledge and application of Constitutional law—rhis possition by liberal justices, his appointees, without Congress's approval/ He has refused to endorse the enactment tort reform e.g. the Obamacare bill, since his final official support in large measure comes from trial lawyers.

5) For imposing taxes on us without our Consent.

6) . . . . For altering fundamentally the Forms of our government.

Since he took office, our President, elected by the free will and choice of the people, he has designed a program that advances not the values of free men, values of honesty in government and probity in public conduct, but he has, instead, concealing his true intentions, driven this nation's debt further into the darkness of total destruction, the economy of a bankrupt people who know not the limits to their capacity to govern with moral discretion and judicious honesty. The people are in rebellion; let the liberal Democrats, in particular, in the Congress beware for as the conservative govenment grows, so will the atttude and power of the people to turn out the offenders from the seats of power. We remain a free people only insofar as we act to unseat the present demagods of power and founders of our astonishing debt produced by greed and the unattentive trust in a great people. We know that our President campagned under false colors . . . as a loyal American. He is loyal, by his own action, to the foreign agenda, the alien ideology of the Marxist state, which is but a short distance from the damnations of political tyranny.

LIBERTY FOR SALE

Taking stonemens bribes his noble oblige slands
This capon of change, gratuitously bought at sale
Cons gulled millions to share his noble slant
Whilest he plays the global currierr lest he fail.

He bruits for's power, arrogant in the breech
Mistakes he the world's envy for his edict's smile
He deems hespreads our wealth mockery in th' breech.
He dips into our pockets. avast his craven guile

Ugly ingrate of history brgiht, he dings default,
Would plead false pity for wanderings afloat
On their envy, indolence and wry rejection' salt
He assails our gleaming history by 's eloquent tout

Strips he our liberties hard won by 's toothesome rant
The easier to make his covey of crooks to recant

PROFIT IS, WHAT?

Mammon is his god, discipled, we share not
Contemptuous of our past, he glories in 's power
Thinking it comes from him, Marx besought.
Condemns he profit s pawn of hidden dowers

This conning well-bred elite, cleansed by cap ideas
Harlequin of change, all tangled in ramcors skeins
He scorns rewards most kind in honor's plea;
Thinking them selflis jills, he spends his means.

This drip of another culture alien to our past
Our struggles, inventions, westward growth so great
Apologetic to evil, our sins into global yaws cast
Yet this icon guts our worth with unnatural pleas for State

He leads us into the maw of death and war sure
For he defends not the stand of liberty pure.

PROFIT PLUS SPECIALIZATION, A PRESIDENT IN DEFAULT

I saw at once that Obama's censure of profit in a post campaign speech that promoted his health care plan and demonzied the insurance industry that such a censure belongs to his ideology. Karl Marx, Obama's mentor, denounced profit as the key to despicable wealth, personal and corporate, which in his fabricated socialist society must be spread about among all members of society. FAIRNSS in the redistribution of wealth, e.g. THE REWARDS FOR LABOR BY OTHERS is the guiding axiom of Obama's Marxism. Poor old Karl Marx! He felt so put upon by London's society, the Fleet Street bond makers and lawyers, the laborite enemies of a just redistribution of British gold! Lies, deceptions, trickery must not stand in the way. Barack Obama has proved the utility of these tools of satan, corrupts cions of the welfare State.

Many years ago, the 1950's, I reviewed a book for Joseph Henry Jackson of the book department at the SF Chronicle. The title of the book was THE ROAD TO SERFDOM, by Hayek. The book has since become a classic. That was the pivotal point in my learning about socialist economy. Therefore, I was prepared for Obama's ploy to eliminate profit by way of his health care plan, under his supposition—the Obama delusion—that the absence of profit will incentivize" the workers toil unjustly for the rich. The word "incentivize" is Obama's word for the destruction of this "unfair" hierarchy.

PROFIT IS CAPITAL AT WORK, to be reinvested in the business or company or service, used to raise wages of employees and enhance the life-styles of all workers, above and beyhond their creation of a service or a producgt that attracts consumers. The formula is so simple! Thornstein

Veblen's "conspicuous consumption," a spinoff of Marxism, is for Barack, not for the "workers of the world", for he has proved he loves money and its affluent properties to the point of his worship of money. He, in fact, is a political engenue of Mollock.

A socialist society is constructed on the supposition that wages only are sufficient for the workers, in satisfaction of their basic survival needs—to each according to his ability. Any enhancements must come from the Federal government in the form of entitlements That tyrannical control of private income of investment plus profits seized by higher and higher taxes for a "public industry" is the power Barack Hussein Obama seeks with his Obamacare bill. He does not give a damn about the sick the aged, the injured, the handicapped. He has proved over and over again that they are impediments to his career advancement insofar as they block passage of his healh care bill. His bill is so inclusive and controlling in the most intimate aspects of our lives that it, the healthcare bill, will, realistically, destroy democratic America. What can be more humanly compelling thanc an our personalcare for our health, intmate, sacrificial, urgent and non-negotiable. Tht is control.

Profit is money acquired bymeans of customer, patron, cllient consumption to the offeror of a service or product—beyond its cost. Obama covets for a gaggle of bureaucrats in DC that so-called "excess." He is convinced that that "excess" should go to the government instead of int the pockets of individual entrepreneurs and their workers. But why? you ask, given that "excess" to bureucrats had no part in its acquisition Envy, greed, lust for power, shame—all are factored in as reasons. ILclude gifts to buddies of Obama. He and his renegade disciples of Big Daddy Government claim that they are smarter than you and therefore his uses for that "excess" rump your uses and are morally and pragmatically superior to your planned uses for that "excess." Barack Obama's only Presidential hope is that ou will flindhappiness and conentment in your work without entreprenur profits, and that you will find increasing joy in working for wages only, without fringe benfits, beonuses, performance increases, job promotions or seasonal gifts, by order of the tyrant of the oligarchy, Barack Obama. Cheers! Try that on professionals in all fields, tricksters of the Left li Congress and the Adminisrtration.

In the 1959's I saw that the wealth created by profit above costs means affluence for the management and the labor of a company, for the individual businessman and his employees. The government under Karl Marx deplores that "excess," that income of consummer money that goes beyond costs. That excess creates the wealth he abhors, although, being a hypocrite, that wealth is an okay emolument for him and Michelle but\ not for Joe the Plummner. To eliminate worker and management profit in order to create better production is delusional. That is the chief delusion of socialism. It is the delusion Barack Obama clings to. European "workers of the world," peons, cannot envisiona a better life because that is the way they are raised, unlike Americans who will not settle for minimun i.e. Federally controlled wages. The Federal Government, this administration, plays the people for fools because they, the people, cherish the concept of reward for labor iln the form of] money they can invest—and by which coms\mption society flourishes. Omitting charitable impulses, what rewards other than money is there that you finely-tailord pieces of liberal political emptiness propose to the Congress as suitable fo your workers Paradise on earth?

The products and inventions and productivity in science, medicine, education are the envy of the world. Obama goes along with their envy and their hatred of America. He is ashamed of our opulence before the world and feels he must apoligize for our visible wealth. His shame we cannot help, since its origin is an old codger in a London Library who invented work without profit as a way of life. Mr. Obama betrays his his ideological upbringing.

But what the contemporary, outspoken pundits omit is specialization. Peons possss no visible talents exceptforeatilng and breeding; the State prefers such abject submission because it preserves them in power. On the other hand, the Doctor of Medicine says:—I can make more profit by the practice of a specialty in medicine. The engineer says:—I can make more money building a better battery, a better prosthesis for medical use, a better dynamo for power plants, a better kind of kitchen ware for busy housewives, a better kind of GPS tractor, milking machine for daiymen . . . All are specialities designed and built by, and sold to meet, a consumer's special need. Marx was an ignoramus about Western society's millions of special needs. Barack Obama 'is equally an ignoramus about 'American society's billions of special needs. He has the imgnationof a ground hog—only one burrow meets his career needs . . . transformation.

In his bill, he woul reduce doctors to general practitioners, because he is essentially an ignorant man. You didn't know that. Many a university graduate walks across that stage knowing less than when he went in, matriculated is the word. How does this shrinking of intelligent enquiry and common-sense wisdom occur—by de-information and, nowadays, by the almost universal doctrine on college and University campuses of political correctness. Obama's health care will destroy our great society of specialiation in all areas of life—the desirable absence of specialition will be extrapolated into, "deemed" useful to education, the insurance industry, banking! Why? Real substantive Specialization generates hideous profits. The Feds must radically curtail profit as an incentive and as a reality. Students will be bullied into conformity lest theylose their Federal student loan! If Obama and his corrupt healthcare bill continue with a life of their own, this nation's great system of advanced education will surely deteriorate and become dismally mediocre with such special subjets being taugh as: "Exploring the Unisex," "Enhancing Your Biodata Card fo rSuccess," "Debt Reduction by Plastic Manipulation," "Spending 101."

Imagine, in banking—no specialization for a bank's consideration of loans! In order to promote an insipid, twisted and unworkable plan to make everybody equal\, regarless of talents or ambition or will, Obama would deliberately degenerate the brilliant innovations and humanitarian contributions of unique individuals by demonizing them as greedy, racists, out of touch. No child is better at math than the next. No man has gifts that exceed the hopes of another. No leader is greater than any other leader in his vision, his abilities. All must be equal, must finish the race at the same time, cannot outshine another. Competition is harmful to the loser, who thereby becomes a victim of a superior-performing, more talentd lindividual. That outlook is stupid, unreal, envious, retrogressive to civiliation and an insult to the people. That sort of egalitarianism is to be imposed on profit-takers and on the creator-contributors, the inventors, the Edisons and all the others who have contributed so profoundly to our society and to the wealth of the world at large. They have no right to fancy themselves superior in a world in which a tryant is trying to impose a false equality.

This nation's wealth is promoted, enlarged, created and invented, made accessble to the world because of its emphasis on specialization. Men and women with special talents contribute to our society because of a specialization they wish to practice. Obama curses this specialization because it leaves out, by-passes the Federal Government and leaves his small soul far behind. He specializes in the destruction of free choice and the liberty to specialize—radical prohibitions layed down by the authority of the Communist Maestro.

To you\ pundits I say—have your airtight case against socialism—and Congratulations on thinking "profit" through. Yet I supply the fool-proof padlock that, by the way, accommodates not just "profit takers." That padlock is SPECIALIZATION. Specialization explains all the myriads of inventions. I supply the chief cause for America's productive diversity—since diversity puts to use talents, as infinitely diverse as is Gods universe. Understand?

To President Obama, I say this:—that nothing in your agenda advances and encourages talents so much as specialization. I think you became a community organizer, first, because you feared the adversarilal environment of the courtroom; then you sorrowed for the poor of East Chicago and you yearned to indulge yourself in the cronyism of your readical leftist mentors. Yet your self-love led you to think you were prepared to lead a great Nation—to adopt the ways of life of Stalin, Hugo Chavez, Tito, Breznev, King George . . . and force the American people by the example of these tyrants, to adopt socialism as a preferred way of life. That suppositious skewering of our two hundred and eleven year old practice of liberty, as a way of life, tells me somethingaout your acuteness of insight, your "vision," your lack of leadership ski\lls. Remove profit by law, and the gifted will refuse to invent, to improve, to explore, to contribute any longer. But you and Axlerod and Holder and Emanuel and your gang of surly, law-breaker advisors are too unaccountably dumb to see the connection between profit and specialization and that inequality of talents that generates true diversity and personally-rewarded (incentivised) achievement.

Your singular and collective lust for power has blinded you to the true genius of America, its creative, inventive genius contributions of the human imagination, the American spirit, the empathy of the American people for the imprisoned, the suffering of the world, driven by the hope of reward, in these instances of fulfillment of compassion's urgency, and then, when the test is material, such as landing on the moon, by the hope for, excuse me, profit to be realized from the specializatio-science of space exploration.

Profilt—reward—that derives from spcialization is the key and the lock to our productive, successful and affluent economy. It draws the world to us. Elinimate that interdependence and you, Obama, will sound the death knell for America's greatness, her springs of inventive genius and her generosity toward the rest of the world in their times of need. Go ahead, you Washington Democrat smart asses. Pass the health care bill . . . but then it may be be too late. Then you will see that as a wise old man who has lived many years and has seen much, I am right on. The people? You have aleady damned the people by controlling them. You damn their basic "social contract," the US Constitution, by fabricating new laws andnew offices without authority, by twisting and warpoing present laws to fit your feelings and the political correctness that substitutes for thought. By your supine benevolence toward the satanic governments of the world that envy this great Nation and its freedom ways of life you weaken our defense. Defense of the people is a primary responsibility of the govenment and the Executive and the Commander-In-Chief of the armed forces. But before the world you curse our defenses as somehow insulting to thoe who would murder our people us and trash our Country. You are therefore useless as as President. You are a preposterous joke on the political scene, sir. It will take them a while to realize that theyhave been suckered in and made fools of, and that they are not the great unwashed masses of Europeanized Americans. You want it both ways, Barack Obama—an affluent life-style and the denial of its honest validity in a free nation.

YOU WERE TAUGHT . . . .

The State, meaning essentially the Federal government, is rapidly taking over the sovereignty of God in the control of the lives of the people in this religion-founded country. Socialism is on the way. Warning.

(1) Parenting by the state is attempting to replace, that is, to clarify values you are taught by instilling the notion of values relativity. There are no absolte values like honor, honesty, courage, respect. Therefore, there can be noteachers of values, no obedience to values for all values are relative to the person,; his lsociety, his culture. Also, social sensitivity has assumed the place in importance over the the three "Rs." even though those curricula teach what is really necessary for gettilng along in society. Feel for each other: thatis of greater importance in life. Let theFederal Government give you instructionson feeling good about others, about situations, complex problems, issus in life. Example: LIfyou feel good about swliping; your card for every purchase,; that is good . . . until your credit-card debt becomes tenthousand dollars. Hmm? Then how do you "feel"?

You are taught that gender does not matter in chosing a life mate. You are also taught—as soldiers were taught with a cucumber in the WWII army—how to put on a condom, and what condoms are for. You are taught that pregnancy can occur at age 14. Any later pregnancy can mess up your life. You are taught that the values of your parents are old-fashioned and out-moded. Strict honesty (who is honest nowadays?), courage (who wants to jump off a clifff?), loyalty (do you think I'm a dog?) can be learned as you grow older. After all, adults do not set examples for you worth your following.

(2) Marriage. You are taught that there are no basic differences between boys and girls, except breasts and genetalia. The Unisex is in, heterosexuality is out. You are taught that it is cool to marry another person of your own gender. You are taucht that society approves of same-sex marriage, and has even passed a law condoning it, withthe blessings of a high priest in a judicial robe who fancviles him self or herself as la qualified spiritual leader. After all, you do not want to be barefoot, in the kitchen with children hanging onto you all the time.

You would pefer to be out smashing rocks with hefty male competitors. Therefore, marry another person of your own gender. You are taught that boys are naturally violent and girls submissive. You are taught that society wants you to reverse these roles, because they are a lie. Adam and Eve are the rmythical characters invented by religionists to promote class warfare, the which they can oversee to their personal gain. You are to stomp our this myth of gender differences, even if you have to join the police, the army, the bomb squad, carry a gun, swear like a drill sargeant and show your manhood as a woman. Let boys keep house—that will take some of the violence out of their natures.

(3) You are taught that partial-birth abortion has its advantages, such as a professional life without the burden of kids. You are taught that the baby is a blob of protoplasm even at birth, and that it does not suffer nearly so much as the doctor and nurses who deliver that blob, suffer from remorse. After all, they are victims of the pro-choice law. You are taught that abortion, by sheer example, has the approval of the people and therefore the approval of God, since we ae a Chrisian nation. A hHigher authority and secular law have become synonymous.

5) You are taught that your parents lack social adjustment education, that they are insensitive to the things, like abortion, boy violence, girl submissiveness (Islam's appeal) and that it is better to take what the teacher says as the truth than what your ignorant parents tell you. If she is a lesbian, let her be your model for courtship. As a matter of fact, since all values are relative, she might just introduce you to the relativism of crimial sex. Criminal? Perish the thought! You are educated to find their values relative to what they want, and you have your wants, also. Differences can always be worked out in a trial court; find a good lawyer.

(6) You are taught that it is wrong to force your religion onto others, so that the elimination of prayers in the classroom, on the school grounds (public property) at graduation, at sports events is good riddance. Then everybody can be happy and satisfied that equality exists. After all wasn't that what the white old men Founders wanted—equality? Well, at last we have it. It took us a long enough time.

(7) You are taught that religion is old-fashioned. It teaches you to hate those who do not believe as you are supposed to believe. It is outmoded and, after all, isn't all justice, relevant to the circumstances?

(8) You are taught that this nation's economy is run by pirates and ne'r-do-wells who want to rob you and your parents, and therefore, it is best to join a group that will speak for you and say, "Enough! We want to take over and show you how to run the country." Elections ae a nuisance. Use whatever prctices—they maybe a little shady—swing the door open for your candidate.

(9) You are taught that outfits like the FCC, chosen by an honorable President, can manage the news best because, like an umpire, they know what fairness means, and they should have the power to enforce the rules and declare penalties. Shut down what offends the majority. Isn't that what democracy is all about—the majority wins?. After all, you believe in following the rules of the fairness game. When your daddy chastened you for some little flaw, he was not being fair. When the teacher gives you a poor grade, she is not being fair. You deserve "A's". Don't let anyone demean you in these ways. You areilmportant, at least to yourself and that's what counts. You deserve to go to college because the President says so. So there! When you are told to do your homework and things like that—the teacher, the school principal, your parents—are not being fair to you. "I have too much homework, and, besides, homewok does nobody any good. Period. It interferes with my favorite TV programs, like "Road to Sucess. Cool"

(10) You are told that the people you see on theTV and hear on the radio tell the truth based on the facts they discover. You cannot prove one way or the other, and so you have to accept their words as truth. After all, they are gettng paid to produce the facts and to give a fair analysis of those facts, are thy not?

(11) When you get big you are going to be rich. When you are rich, everybody likes you and you like to be liked. When you are poor, people discrimate against you. When you are rlch, you are a cool winner in a democracy, since your money speaks for your talent, your traits, (they call character), and your accomplishments in life. You are told, also, that when your father gave you money, he expected you to handle it with good common sense, but that you didn't have to account to him for the way you spent it. That was barging in on your privacy . . . like barging in on your TV in you room. After all, isn't that the way our country runs? We give folks in Washington our money, but we are not their daddy, so do not ask them how they spent it.

The State is now gaining sovereighty over the next generation and, ultimately, the socialist State will emerge in which fallible, corrupt politicians, in and out of the Congress, will dictate to the people how their money, now athe politicians', will be "well spent," without questions, just as their daddys raised them. No questions, please. You are not my daddy with that $1.4 trillion I gave to The the banks, the car companies, the schools and insurance companies . . . Expensive dinners, first class three-month, multiple vacations, expensive air flights, and personal perks We learned in our childhood how to spend the taxpayers money without accountability, yet with good common sense. Sure you did. We do not question you—until we run out of money.

Farewell, Democracy. Bye-bye individual freedoms to chose responsibly. We are all victims of "the system." Have pity on us.
Europe never has those worries. They are free . . . . to vacation half a year.

THE WHITEWASHED SEPULCHRE

There is a verse, Mathew 23:27 that begins:: "Woe to you . . ." Woe does not mean hardships, bad luck. I means a curse upon . . . . Woe (a curse) unto you, Scribes and Pharisees, hypocrites! For you are like whitewashed sepulchres, which on the outside appear beautiful, but inside they are full of dead men's bones and all uncleanliness.

Transliterated for your guidance, the verse means: (Woe) A curse upon you media and politicians, bureaucrats! For you are like whitewashed tombs, which on the outside appear beautiful, with parties, soirees, trips, glistening speeches and photo-opts, but on the inside are full of dead men's bones, Marx, Lenin, Trotsky, and all uncleanliness, as Saul Alinsky propaganda and Eric Bender deceits.

You do not deceive the majority of Americans by your ideologic niceness and your fanfare of self-advertisement as if purified by an alien ideology. You are an American in name only, Mr. Obama, as you continue to practice the Europeanization of our great Nation for selfish ambition. Your squander of $375 thousands of dollars of taxpayer money to send Michelle to Spain on a "vacation" does not deceive us. Her vacation is your writeoff, since it is plausible that she goes there on a mission to rediscover Franco's civil War implictions for America, to objectify our Teaparty movement against Democrat Radicalism in ever-bigger government . . . and to watch the Hemminway bull fIghts iln oder to learn of gladiator courage, useful to you, and how the torreador uses the red cape (of Job, job, jobs) to avoid the bull's (conservative) horns.

We, not you, Barack Obama, are the generous ones. Yours is the spirit of stinginess and deprivation toward us, a charade of charity, whom you dislike with an engaging diffidence for our prosperity, believing that properity to be a rip-off of the rest of the world. You are a deliberately ignorant snob, sir, a disgrace to the office of President! You do not understand our mettle or our faith in ourselves as individuals . . . or in God, the great Provider and source of our liberties. You eschew—not a sneeze but a word—the Declaration of Independence and in its place you would install the Preamble to the Communist Manifiesto, thinking thereby to correct a 200-year old misconception about our country. to wit, that we have inalienable rights protected by our Constitution (not by the State). You think to gradually train us to like your brand of Big Brother is Watching. You promote and engage in tyranny, by videos to the classrooms of America, by your glorified, lying manipulation of your failed policies with language to cause them to appear as successes. Failure will morph into Succss by your use of the courts to legislate changes in policies, the better to cause the people to conform to your socialist control. By your feeble accolades to Ameica's Greatness, you apologizing for that greatness to our enemies so as to cause them to feel better and themselves, we being taken down a notch or two.

You would add to these pusillanimous policies your desire that America appears impotent to produce any more than equivalent retaliation militariily against any nuclear attack by an enemy such as North Korea, a nation state totally bereft of any moral, ethical and politically wise conduct whatsoever. You think to embellish your image by egalitarianism that puts this nation at real risk before a world that distrusts us without cause. Your politics smack of a schizoid personality, sir.

ou find the US Constitution to be a blockade to your ravenous ambition, not to lead the Amercan people but to bamboozle them so as to make a place for yourself in history. Nuts! That is my answer. You are inexplicably inferior intellectually and socially to our Founding Fathers, President Obama. Face it. You detest and denegrate them because they owned property and slaves. You occupy the office of President by the consent of the people's majority, a law established by "those greedy old white men" in Philadelphia, not by your seizure of or right to office. or by any inevitable ascension. Your condemnation is among the bones and uncleaniliness in your whited sepulchure of Presiential charisma.

THE JUDICIAL LEGISLATORS
REPLACE CONGRESS

Supreme Court Nominee Elena Kagan's support of the basic document of law, the fundamental law in America in the "living constitution" is a flawed opinion. She is certainly a "Washington insider," though what that has to do with California I cannot guess. She is full of laughter, "feels comfortable in her own skin, though what that has to do with the law is anyone's guess. She is judicious not to anwer questions that are based on a predictable judgement, though that kind of moot questioning is the only reasonably certain way of getting at her basic understanding of the law and the quality of her judgement and the orientation of her political stance.

Whenever "changing circumstances" are the measure of a law's purpose and the framers' intention, then circumstances drive the judicial interpretation. When that occurs. law becomes mere opinion and the "living Constitution" becomes a changing document of judicial personal opinion, the meanings of which in particular circumstances, are shaped and controled by the justice's personal opinions. This slow erosion of law converts the original constitution into a living document of personal opinons in the guise of law. Such basic changes make a mockery of the law.

The arguments by the liberal court are used to shape the law to fit the conclusion of the radical liberal justices. There can, therefore, be no judicial objectivity. The slant-opinionated law becomes subjective law and ls therefore useless when the circumstances again change, requiring a new subjective analysis of the facts and a new shaping of the meaning of the Constitutional statement-text to fit the facts of the new set of circumstances. This changeability accorded to ourConstiltution converts the US Constiltutionas foundation lawm, vital to the survival of this nation, moot, transient, unreliaibleand suspect.

Think about that, citizen. That politicization of the Contitution—and that is what it is by leftist justices—ui judical opportunism that can lead to all sorts of corruption and personal vendettas and preconditions established by the Suprome Court to bring the law under their personal control, instead of the reverse.

This adjustment of the Constitutional prohibitions to the interdictions of human preferences is also a form of Judicial Dictatorship, not to be confused with the rule of law but, intead, it is the rule of men in a court of law. Law has become opinion. Authority has become man-based opportnism instead of law-based necessity. The higher law becomes a form of judicial activism, God endowed rights becomeltransient and the moral and ethicals security of a people trembles beforethe indecisions of activsist jurists . . .

In Kagan's case, this politization makes way for Obama's opinionated agenda, regardless of any protections of the law now established in the Constiltution—a document to constrain the three branches of government, desssilgned to make them separate but equal arms, and to protect the people from robbery of their rights BY ANY ONE BRANCH of the government. If she has her way, Kagan's "living constiltution" will then no longer be a Constitution of laws fothe governing and for protection of he America people. Instead, it will have become a document that glorifies and enforces leftist and liberal agenda objectives, in a word—that justify its very existence. The people willlhve becomnelcaptives sof the radical Left andsubjects, not ccitizens, of State Socialism.

Kagan's view of the living Constitution makes out fallible (Statist) man to appear infallible, unmistaken in his decisions, and givers of all good to society, virtuous beyond criticism and the salvationist branch of government, with its swarm of agencies, for the improvement of fallible men in our society . . . therefore, we are stupid not to accept the Statist-god's gifts, but we can be enlightened by our masters in government—the bureaucrats and voice supreme, Barack Hussein Obama.

The "living constlituion" concept makes way for the government to control all aspects of our lives, a far more insidious doctrine than the docrine of subject-control imposed by king and Parliament. A vote for Kagan is a vote for the destruction of America by way of the destruction of the purpose, meaning and efficacy of its fundamental document of enlightment, protection and authority, the US Constitution. Obama by his appointment intends to morph America into a nation of third-world illusory prosperity and tryanny of control over our lives and the lives of our posterity. This is he doctrine of Statist retribution, a form of benign yet crippling vengeance against America chiefly because of her wealth and leadership before the world.

Remember his ignorant view of our history: We are now headed "in the right direction." economically. That is the socialist illusion he wishes to project. I fear that before he is out of office, we will discover him to be the dirty little sociaiist dictator that is actually is. I predict he will attempt to control educatio in the lower grades, especially by means of educational tele-lessons from Washington. And that all programs of community supported colleges willlbe forced to pass throughs the arbitration of a Washington DOE board, greatly enlarged. The Christian church will be next by the installation. for the first time in our history of of taxation not upon churches but upon their parking spaces and media time and, obstructively, on conditional salaries of pastors.

His view of America's history is based on the "rules" and tactics of the Alinsky and Marx model of Europe's Medieval society. This pathetic analysis of America's colonial past imputes serfdom to the colonists. They were serfs, in our Colonial days/ We tilled the land under a king and his Parliament. We viewed freedom before and after the Revolution as a necessary exploitation of the poor of the world. We sucked the wealth and vitality from the rest of suffering mankind, especially from Europe in order to achieve our great merchantile society. Obama would now show us the true meaning of freedom by his anarchistic tyranny, the raping of institutions of their wealth and control, punishing our labor with regulations like a Medieval baron. He would create a permanently dependent underclass to keep his kind in power, dependent on the Federal governmen with handouts, entitlements and destructive taxes, animated by an ongoing class envy of "the rich," the bar ever lowering to accommodate his Marxist Ideology. Marxismand Christian ilty are inconsistent,despite the arguments of the liberation theology, the Rev. Wright;s philosophy and Obama's attractant for twenty years. The one worhips Jesus Christ, the other worships man's works.

His plan is diabolical for this great country, the work of a Hollywood-type charismatic demagogue. Our mistake, of conservatives, is to assume that he accepts yet distorts the true American history. Idealogue President Obama is the result of a warp of lies by his leftist trainers. His promissory lies put him in power. He is missing something, however. We are not bound to the the Federal government in helpless illusory post-industrial servitude. We, the people and not himself, are the source of his power. We do not find either himself, his administration or the Congress or the State to be virtuous. The true and only God almighty is virtuous. From His hands came the gift of this great nation!

CONCSCIENCES OF DOCTORS

And now one of Obama's defunct policies is to overturn, if that is the word, the Supreme Court's recognition of the conscience of a doctor who refuses to perform an abortion, early or late term. That fraud in the White House has not read Paul's letter (I) to the Corinthians in which he (10: 5, 27, 28) admonishes them that his freedom is not to be judged by another's conscience."\ What makes your conscience so special, Obma, that you should expunge the consciences of medical doctors and force them by law to wound their consciences by disobedience. In other words, what special demon of hell do you represent, Barack Obama, that would rebuke Almighty God's protection of doctors' consciences in their respect forhuman life? Hmmm? You may be out of the reach of the people if you make this policy law, but you are not out of the reach of the God the Creator!

HIDDEN BIODATA CARD CHAINS

Hidden from view, until it is revealed by open Fedeal enforcement, is a little—known provison in the 1000 + page Obamacare bill that takes the American people prisoner of the Central Socialist Government: The provision mandates, by Obamalaw and Leftist insinuations, that all Americans are protected by carrying about with them at all times a BIODATA CARD. The media agitprop thrust is that this protects the people from the influence of and encroachments of illegal aliens. Here are the real provisions of the BIODATA CARD: Present to the requesting authority your-DNA, blood type, retina scan, fingerprints, and, as coming attractions, your religion, ethnicity, occupation, bank, income, marital status, children, diseases, handicaps, political party, and, oh yes, date of birth. These data will disciminate you from illegals. With this card, you will be qualified to live in Amerca. Happy? Thrilled to death? Remember: now that you are dogs whose lives are controlled by Washington elites, ou have no rights except by their toleration. God-given rights? The Constitution? History? What in hell are you talking about?

You will have to show this card to board an airplane, a train or steamship. You will have to show this card to purchase groceries at a state market. You will have to show this card to apply for any job, to enter an educational institution, to apply for a loan of any sort, to get married, or contract lawfully for a home, enterprise, or to settle a traffic court pleading. The Federal Government will have access to your bank account and the capacity to withdraw funds without your knowldge or approval in case you are in any way, shape or form in default . . . in their bueaucrat opinion!

This BIODATA CARD will, in reality, be the key to your imprisonment by the Federal Government, courtesy of the slick tongued, incorrigible liars who belong to Socialist-Marxist Barack Obama. He owns quite a kennel of these wicked perpetrators of socio-political powes. It is we who will serve him and his power-lusting disciples. Start with video propaganda to school kids!

You will bear "the mark ot he beast." At first it will be an onerous thought, then the BIODATA card, and then a Federal ID chip embedded somwhere on your person, as for a lost dog that can be found. You will be found, all right. The link to this BIODATA CARD is a nationl Police State, since all of this intimate data will be transferred to a master Police master file. This will be the European police-state in action. If a finance company cannot track your "bar code" chip, the benign Gestapo will commence their search. They have your number. for sure. This chip will become a bar code of the State's devising.

A majority of you put this demon-activated, wicked man in the service of satan, into the highest office in our land. He misled you by his unconscionable lies and pretentions to servanthood. But what's done is done. I am nobody except before God. I have no political clout. I would not have a platform for my voice but for this computer—even now the dogs n DC have their eye on the internet to squelch it as an opposing force. Yet I am warning you that unless you rid the nation of this felon in disguise, this maniac anarchist Obama (what Constitution, taking with him his wicked and perverse cohorts in the Congress and in the administration, you will get more than a thrill up your leg in 2014 and in years to come. You will be prisoners in actuality of the State, serfs managed by the DC barons of power. It is up to you. Your weapon of defensive attack is your vote.

Do not listen to the know-nothing, silenced idiots in the Media. Those Pravda illiterates are incapable of joining two consecutive thoughts together. They are gone, dead, irretrievable vestiges of a once great liberty-loving, figting media. They belong to the State. The media are now the property of the State, a Soviet style Agitprop, agitating propagandists who promote the radical, Marxist, elitist agenda by this President. Now they are the performing marionettes with strings controlled by the socialist boyking in the White House. As for the Lincoln Memorial crowd, half a million Americans can't all be wrong.

Life, liberty and the pursuit of happiness are inconsistent with the Federally ordered BIODATA CARD. It is coming, signed into law by a man of perverse lips named Barack Hussein Obama, god of the dumbed-down media sychophants. The bottom line is that all these things are not necessary in a presently free society. The smell-rotten gang in Washington wants power to control your life. Throw the ideological bastards out, cynical whelps fathered by the spirits of darkness to destroy America, land of the free.

WASHINTON SPENDTHRIFTS

So long as Washington Spendthrifts control the purse-strings, an audit of their profligate squandering is admirably in order. My one concern is that distrubution of the records of unaccounted for swag will not be included, small comfort to conservaives and a corpulent sigh of relief to the prodigals of the Left. They have owned American generosity, they have stuffed their pockets with taxpayer loot, they have promised the demons from Marxist college grand reembursements for nothing that benefits us who foot their damned spending-spree programs. So again, an audit will speak to the heart of the runaway spending, but, I ask, will the fortuitous members of Congress be so agile as to pass only cursory notice on the audit. What will follow the audit, now that the pirates—who sift through the cherished moneys gained by Americans' hard work—consider themselves the elite of the domain. Will they recant of their loose ways with our dollars? Are there any penalties if some corruptions on the left are discovered, the briggands having stolen into the House chamber at midnight to rob the people. Let us hope they will recan and show signs of thrift-mangement. I will watch the flight of HR 1207, and congratulatir thoe Representative who show the spsirit, insight and fortitude to co-author the bill, the Federal Reserve Transparency Act. There are not many whom we can trust in Washington nowadays.

www.ingramcontent.com/pod-product-compliance
Lightning Source LLC
Chambersburg PA
CBHW020334290526
45785CB00005B/2008